STORMING THE GATES OF HELL

By Des Griffin

*Dedicated to, among others, Margaret Macdonald,
John Darby, C.I. Scofield, Hal Lindsey,
the glib-tongued throng of TV Evangelists,
and my local community church friends —
without whom the inspiration to write this book
would have been considerably diminished.*

***

Copyright© by Emissary Publications, 1996
9205 SE Clackamas Rd., #1776, Clackamas OR 97015

Printed in the United States of America
ISBN: 0-941380-07-6

All rights reserved. No part of this book may be reproduced in any form without permission, in writing, from the publisher, except by a reviewer who wishes to quote brief passages in connection with a review in a magazine or newspaper.

ABOUT THE AUTHOR

Des Griffin is the author of *Fourth Reich of the Rich* (1976), *Descent Into Slavery?* (1980), *Martin Luther King: The Man Behind the Myth* (1987), and *Anti-Semitism and the Babylonian Connection* 1988. He is also the editor of *Midnight Messenger.* This bi-monthly publication brings its readers behind the scenes, and into the real world of politics, economics, and human affairs.

A long-time student of national and international affairs, Des Griffin has written numerous articles on a wide variety of subjects. His articles have appeared in *Midnight Messenger* and in various publications, both in the United States and overseas. He is well known for his painstaking research and documentation. Mr. Griffin is a frequent guest on nationwide talk-shows.

Des Griffin, a citizen of the United States, has lived and worked in Ireland, England and Canada. He has been an avid researcher and student of the Bible for some forty years. He has traveled widely.

TABLE OF CONTENTS

Chapter 1
Insanity Reigns — 1
Chapter 2
The Principle of Cause and Effect — 5
Chapter 3
What Do You Mean By "Government"? — 10
Chapter 4
What Is Man? — 20
Chapter 5
Satan's Plan: A Masterpiece of Diabolical Ingenuity — 34
Chapter 6
Man: A Natural Conspirator — 45
Chapter 7
Global Overview? — 59
Chapter 8
Top Secret Agreement — 69
Chapter 9
White Supremacists Exposed — 79
Chapter 10
What do You Mean, Christianity? — 90
Chapter 11
The Great American Pastor Disaster — 95
Chapter 12
The Abrahamic Covenant — 108
Chapter 13
The Abrahamic Covenant Today — 116
Chapter 14
Biblical Christianity — 124
Chapter 15
The New Testament Church — 136
Chapter 16
The New Covenant And The 70 Weeks Prophecy — 154
Chapter 17
The Big Showdown — 191
To Stand Alone — 182
Encouraging The Remnant — 183

INTRODUCTION

REALITY!

When I was born I knew nothing — zip! I was helpless. I had no knowledge, no understanding, and even less wisdom. Come to think of it, I was positively "dumb." (Some people doubt if the latter has really changed!).

Following my birth, I would have lain within inches of my first meal and died of malnutrition and dehydration were it not for the fact that my mother or a nurse had compassion on me and directed me to where food was available. Even then I was probably so lacking in discernment that they may well have had to "work my lips" in order to show me how to gain nourishment. It wasn't exactly an inspiring performance!

I did, however, learn quite fast. By my teenage years, I was pretty confident that I "had it all together." I was brash and cocky; I was convinced that I knew it all. What a magnificent talent!

Then something traumatic occurred. That Tuesday early in 1954 had been one of the most enjoyable days of my young life. Everything had gone perfectly. With two friends, I drove to a town some fifty miles from where we lived. There, we spent the afternoon at the racetrack betting on the horses.

Later, we spent part of our winnings on a lavish meal. No expense barred! We then headed for the local dog track. Our luck held. We had a ball. We were on top of the world! This was where the "action" was! Truly, this was what the Italians call "Dolce Vita," the Good Life! We were exhilarated. We sang and joked all the way home.

When I finally sat down on the edge of my bed in the small hours of the following morning, I was feeling great. As I began to get ready for bed, I reviewed the exciting events of the previous day. Suddenly, without warning, my whole world fell apart, collapsing in ruins all around me. The truth hit me like a bolt of lightning. My life was empty — totally lacking in substance.

I was immediately engulfed by a dark cloud of frustration and despair. My life, my activities, my thoughts, and my interests all dissolved in an explosion of irrelevance. They no longer appeared to have any real meaning or purpose; they were exposed as threadbare and worthless. My dream-world lay in shambles, my false images smashed into millions of meaningless pieces.

This was my first head-to-head, eyeball-to-eyeball confrontation with reality. It revealed a devastating emptiness in my life!

As Winston Churchill once observed, "Most people, sometime in their lives, stumble across the truth. Most jump up, brush themselves off, and then hurry on about their business as if nothing had happened."

That is what I did — at least on the surface. I hurried on about my business (my personal emptiness) as if nothing had happened! I never told anyone about my traumatic experience until many years later.

However, deep down in my heart-of-hearts nothing was to be the same again. A basic change had *begun* to take place in my life. This ego-shattering experience was quickly followed by a long visit to a hospital; as a result of developing TB of the spine — a relatively rare disease — I was confined to bed in a plaster cast for some fifteen months. Initially that, too, was a devastating experience! How could all this possibly be happening to me? It just didn't make sense!

For the first time, I was forced to ask important questions — and seek serious answers. What was this thing called "life" all about? Was there any real purpose to it? If so, what was that purpose? Could it be discovered?

And how about the world around me? It seemed so filled with problems and complex contradictions as to be beyond comprehension. And world affairs, did they have any rhyme or reason? It seemed not!

Unknown to me at the time, I was on my way to making some of the most amazing and wonderful discoveries of my life — the uncovering of knowledge and understanding that, in the decades that followed, would totally revolutionize my life and eventually lead to the writing of this book.

Now, read on....

Chapter 1

INSANITY REIGNS

As the United States races at breakneck speed towards the end of the twentieth century, our once great nation finds itself floundering in the midst of an immense storm-ravaged ocean of crime, drugs, debauchery, human decadence, moral depravity, pornography, purposelessness, and debt. In a flight of national insanity unparalleled in the annals of human history, our leaders have in recent decades systematically sabotaged our ship of state and thrown overboard the guide book, the compass, and the anchors that were instrumental in guiding us with spectacular success since our initial launching in 1776. Truly, there is no soundness to be found from the top of our heads to the soles of our feet. There are only "wounds and bruises, and putrefying sores; they have not been closed, neither bound up, neither mollified with ointment" (*Isaiah* 1:6).

"Except the Lord of hosts had left unto us a very small remnant we should have been as Sodom, and we should have been like unto Gomorrah" (v.9).

As our sick society plummets ever closer to its doom, a cacophony of conflicting voices cry out in the midst of the raging storm of confusion vying at every point of the compass for our attention. The masses, tossed to and fro by every wind of doctrine, first have their hopes raised and then dashed amidst the babble of bewilderment that presently dominates the American scene. Most people, with a reckless attitude of "posterity be damned," have thrown aside the few strands of morality and personal responsibility that remain in American society and plunged headlong into the smorgasbord of demonic delights with which they are surrounded: "Let's get ours while the getting is good."

The churches which, in yesteryear, were the pillars upon which our productive, powerful, vibrantly alive, and immensely wealthy republic was built, have — in all too many cases — abandoned any semblance of sound moral and spiritual leadership. They have now degenerated into little more than social clubs; in services, members are entertained but never trained to face reality and do battle with the enemy.

As was true in every great civilization of the past, there are those few dauntless souls who brave the scorn and ridicule of their shipmates; they "cry aloud and spare not," they warn of imminent peril if our ship's course is left uncontrolled and its crew unchecked. Except in rare cases such cries of alarm fall on deaf ears.

UNLEARNED LESSONS

History is replete with lessons unlearned and warnings unheeded; one of the more bizarre quirks of human nature is that it just refuses to be confused with the facts! And, as philosopher George Santayana once observed, those who ignore the lessons of history are doomed to repeat them.

As what has publicly passed for Christianity has declined in prestige and influence, another worldwide movement — the New Age phenomenon — has shown tremendous growth in both popularity and influence. Multiple millions believe that this growing phenomenon holds the key to the future well-being of not only our nation but also the world. In unison with the New Agers, politicians around the globe cry out for the creation of a New World Order or one world government — "a new world, a new philosophy, and new relationships.... Let us all coalesce with all our strength, mind, heart, and soul around a New Genesis, a true global, God-abiding political, moral and spiritual renaissance to make this planet at long last what it was always meant to be: the Planet of God" (*New Genesis: Shaping a Global Spirituality*, by Robert Muller).

WHAT IS MEANT BY, NEW AGE?

What is meant by, New Age? As pointed out in a pamphlet by author John Daniel, "The answer is found in astrology, whose adepts teach that there exists a time clock in the night sky called the zodiac. This great turning wheel of twelve constellations makes a complete rotation approximately every 24,000 years. Each of the twelve constellations, therefore, has ascendancy over the skies of the earth for about 2,000 years. According to the ancient Babylonian astrologers, as each new constellation arrives a "new age" is born, accompanied by a catastrophic or otherwise crucial event on the earth.

"Modern mystics of the current New Age movement claim that the crucial event that ushered in the age of Pisces (the Fishes) two thousand years ago was the birth of Jesus Christ. Hence, in the year 2,000, when Pisces succumbs to the ascendancy of Aquarius, we can expect — according to the New Agers — that Christianity will cease to exist and mankind will take a 'quantum leap' into godhood, the final cycle of evolution."

THE AGE OF AQUARIUS

Advocates declare that the Age of Aquarius will sweep away all the old, archaic, and horribly restrictive rules and regulations that have held the human race in bondage from time immemorial; humankind will thus be freed from the curse of guilt and fear imposed upon it by Christianity and the Bible. The New Age of Aquarius will exalt the "brotherhood of man," thus allegedly ushering in a millennium of unprecedented peace and prosperity. In this wonderful world of tomorrow, as in the fairy tales of old, every one will live happily ever after.

Humanly speaking, it is very easy to see how one could be swept up in the euphoria of such utopian dreams; the idea of playing a role in the creation of a new dream-world certainly appeals to people's innate desire to be part of something that exalts them above the ordinary. It's a heavy trip.

In the final analysis, however, there is only one problem with such a plan — it is based on a damnable lie, the same shop-worn and dog-eared old lie that Satan pawned off on Eve in the Garden of Eden ... "Ye shall be as gods" (*Genesis* 3:5). Yes, the twenty-first century New Age dream of creating a New World Order is but a modern version of the same old Satanically-inspired Babylonian dream of "making a name for themselves" by creating a one world government (*Genesis* 11:4). In their demented vanity, these people really believe they can kick God (the Eternal Creator) off His throne, push Him out of the way, bury what one of their spokesmen, John Dunphy, calls "the rotting corpse of Christianity," and run the show themselves. Old Babylon or New Age — the aim's the same!

Make no mistake about it, modern New Agers have the same attitude as Lucifer (or Satan): "[We] will ascend into heaven. [We] will exalt [our] throne above the stars of God ... [We] will ascend above the heights of the clouds; [We] will be like the most High" (*Isaiah* 14:13,14).

As the Preacher said, "there is no new thing under the sun. Is there anything whereof it may be said, See, this is new? it hath been already of old time...." (*Ecclesiastes* 1:9,10).

Their diabolical plans failed at the time of Ancient Babylon; they will surely fail again!

Chapter 2

THE PRINCIPLE OF CAUSE AND EFFECT

How was it possible for such a diabolical philosophy to gain such a stranglehold in America? How could our nation which, in the words of Abraham Lincoln, had been the recipient of "the choicest blessing of heaven" have descended so far so quickly? How could America, which had "grown in numbers, wealth and power as no other nation had ever grown ... have forgotten the gracious Hand which preserved us in peace and multiplied and enriched and strengthened us?"

How did our once fabled "land of the free and home of the brave" become, in just a few short decades, the world's leading purveyor of everything that would have been a stench in the nostrils of our founding fathers? What caused the devastating effects that dominate every stratum of American society as we come to the conclusion of another millennium? Why are our nation's present leaders so intent upon surrendering our national sovereignty? Why are they shackling the chains of slavery on the backs of the American people? Why are they pushing so enthusiastically for creation of a New World Order?

The answers to these and many other questions need to be addressed — **and understood** — by every American. To do so, we need to apply the biblical truth that "whatsoever things were written aforetime were written for our learning" (*Romans* 15:4). Only when we rigorously apply this principle in every phase of our personal lives will we begin to sort out fact from fiction, reality from illusion. Only then will we be in a position to make informed, sane, and logical decisions in our everyday lives. Unless and until we come to the point where we can view the Big Picture of national and world affairs with knowledge and understanding — *from both a biblical and secular perspective* — we will continue to be helplessly tossed to and fro on the ocean of life like so much flotsam and jetsam. Those who find themselves in such a position will increasingly become the helpless pawns of others who wish to work their wicked will upon the human race under the diabolical guise of the One World/New Age philosophy.

CHRISTIAN NATION

Early American history provides abundant proof that the Colonies were founded on God's Law and biblical principles; from the beginning the Bible was the basic law book. Colonial society was solidly founded on biblical law and the principles of individual self-government, personal responsibility, hard work, integrity, a closely-knit family unit — and a total conviction in the sovereignty of God.

The awesome responsibility that this fact placed on the early settlers was voiced by John Winthrop (1588-1649), a leader in the Massachusetts colony: "We shall be as a city on a hill. The eyes of all people are upon us, so if we shall deal falsely with our God in this work we have undertaken and so cause Him to withdrew His present help from us, we shall be made a story and a by-word throughout the world."

The fact that America was founded as a basically "Christian nation" was emphasized by Justice J. Brewer in an address delivered at Harvard in 1905. Brewer referred to Supreme Court cases, both state and federal, and many state documents and constitutions. In conclusion, he stated: "In no charter or constitution is there anything to even suggest that any other than the Christian is the religion of this country.... In short, there is no charter or constitution that is either infidel, agnostic or non-Christian....

"Christianity came to this country with the first colonists; has been powerfully identified with its rapid development, colonial and national, and today exists as a mighty factor in the life of the Republic. This is a Christian country and we can rejoice" (*United States: Christian Nation*, The Christian Committee, Lakemore, Ohio).

"AFLAME WITH RIGHTEOUSNESS"
When French philosopher/statesman Alexis De Tocqueville came to America in 1830 he sought to find the source of our national greatness. He searched far and wide, without success. It was only when he visited America's churches and found them "aflame with righteousness" that his quest proved successful. Those churches loudly proclaimed the Sovereignty of God, the Lordship of Jesus Christ and the inerrancy of Scripture; they were instrumental in transforming the lives of multiple millions and in educating and equipping them to do battle against the forces of evil. The "salty" Christians (*Matthew* 5:13) produced under such marvelous conditions served as a powerful preserving agent throughout the great American Republic. During the same period, all levels of the education system — be it at a local school or university level — were fundamentally biblical in nature and thrust. In fact, Harvard College (later university) was founded in 1636 to, among other things, promote the Christian religion. It was named in honor of John Harvard, a Puritan preacher.

The prosperity and well-being of the United States wasn't an accident. It was mainly a matter of cause and effect; the effect was caused by a reverence for and a response to the laws and principles clearly laid out in God's word. "Righteousness exalteth a nation: but sin is a reproach to any people" (*Proverbs* 14:34).

But around the 1830s the overall situation began to slowly change — on a variety of fronts. At the scholastic level, American students who attended the leading universities of Europe returned to the United States having imbibed heavily of the heady wine of German Rationalism. With their degrees in education from Europe's institutes of "higher learning," they began to fill important positions in American universities; thus began the steady erosion of academic standards in our leading institutions of higher learning.

The basic tenets of the new educational philosophy were contrary to everything that had served to make America a giant among the pygmies of the world. Operating from the basic premise that all religious convictions are both false and foolish, and could be easily explained away through human reason, the new philosophy openly attacked most established beliefs (*History of Rationalism*, by Hurst, p.27). One Rationalist leader arrogantly announced that "the turning point in history will be the moment man becomes aware that the only God of man is man himself" (*Atheistic Humanist*, by de Lubec, p.10). Yet another source defined Rationalism as "that manner of thought by which human reason is considered to be the only source and the only judge of all kinds of knowledge" (*De Rationalism*, by Hahn).

In the years that followed, the educational philosophy known as Rationalism attracted or spawned many individuals and groups that were instrumental in spreading and popularizing its God-denying, Christ-defying, man-exalting tenets. Charles Darwin (1809-1882) was one such person. Darwin's greatest contributions to the further "rationalization" and corruption of mankind were his two most popular books — *Origin of the Species* (1859) and *The Descent of Man* (1871). In them, Darwin attempted to explain creation without a Creator, life without a Lifegiver, design without a Designer, law without a Lawgiver, and the continuing existence of the universe without a Sustainer.

Although his assertions and alleged "scientific findings" were anything but truly scientific — and in a sense made monkeys out of men — they did have a major and long-lasting impact on American society. They provided an apparently rational basis upon which rebellious man could "do his own thing" without running afoul of an Omnipotent, Just and Law-Enforcing Creator.

The fact that such rationalizations didn't work in the time of Noah, in the days of Sodom and Gomorrah, and certainly haven't since the publication of Darwin's two "masterpieces," seems to have conveniently escaped the attention of the self-appointed experts who presently occupy top positions in the fields of science and academia. However, that fact should hardly surprise us. You see, hope dwells eternal in the hearts of carnal man!

It is interesting to note that practically all the individuals who fancy themselves as experts on the theory of evolution and related subjects — and whose alleged virtues have been repeatedly extolled in the pages of "highly respected scientific journals" — now adamantly refuse to even discuss the matter in public. They may realize deep down in their hearts that the very basis of their life's work has been exposed as threadbare and completely lacking in substance, yet they still cling to their error with the tenacity of a bulldog; some are tenured professors at the nation's most prestigious universities. To publicly admit their error and foolishness would be an ego-shattering experience of gargantuan proportions; it could be so psychologically disruptive that the ego destruction could lead to a mental breakdown.

Their predicament is perhaps best summed up by Jesus Christ: "[T]his is the condemnation, that light is come into the world, and men loved darkness rather than light, because their deeds were evil.

"For every one that does evil hates the light, neither comes to the light, lest his deeds be reproved.

"But he that does truth comes to the light, that his deeds may be made manifest that they are wrought in God" (*John* 3:19-21).

Is it any wonder, then, that these self-appointed leaders of the masses so adamantly refuse to allow their ideas to be discussed and examined in an open forum? Instead of being open and truthful, they sneer and jeer at — and ridicule — those who ask honest questions and seek answers to the major questions of life; in their spiritual bankruptcy and moral depravity, they cling to and hide behind darkness lest their phoniness and deceitfulness be exposed for all to see. As Scripture says, "The heart is deceitful above all things and desperately wicked: who can know it?" (*Jeremiah* 17:9).

It is important that we recognize that nothing happens in a vacuum. Things don't "happen" accidentally. On whatever level — be it personal, spiritual, academic, economic, political, etc. — there are causes for every effect.

In the pages that lie ahead, we shall take a close look at the **effects** that we see all around us in today's world; then, we will examine — from both a biblical and a secular perspective — the **causes** that brought them about.

Chapter 3

WHAT DO YOU MEAN BY "GOVERNMENT"?

From the dawn of time one problem has towered above all others in the long and sordid history of mankind; that problem is government. Over the approximately 6,000 years of human history, mankind — both individually and collectively — has experimented with every conceivable type and variation of government — and has, with two brief possible exceptions, failed miserably to achieve anything remotely resembling true peace and prosperity.

The present massive international drive to create a New World Order is just the latest of innumerable efforts down through the centuries from the time of Nimrod's Babylon. It, too, will fail — though much more ignominiously than all its predecessors. With that event, man will finally learn the lesson of the Ages — that, contrary to the Satanic lie (*Genesis 3:5*), he is not "as God" and is therefore totally incapable of achieving world peace by his own efforts.

MOST BASIC QUESTION

From the time of creation, the most basic of all questions has been, who makes the rules? Who is it that determines what is right and what is wrong? Who determines the laws and principles that govern our everyday affairs — both as individuals and as a society — if we are to reach our fullest potential as human beings? Who's the Boss — God or man?

For mankind as a whole, that question was decided in the Garden of Eden. There, Eve (with Adam standing quietly by her side) believed the serpent's lie that they could be their own "god" and, in true democratic style, make up their own rules. Eve found it attractive; it appealed to her pride and vanity, and she fell for the bait — hook, line and sinker. This first experiment in democracy (man makes the rules) ended in catastrophe. More on this later. The rest is history — and all down hill.

"THE WICKEDNESS OF MAN WAS GREAT"

As earth's population grew and expanded, things went from bad to worse. Man's experiment in making up his own rules — in wilful defiance of his Maker and Lawgiver — had a very predictable outcome: "And God saw that *the wickedness of man was great* in the earth, and that *every* imagination of the thoughts of *his* heart was only evil continually" (*Genesis* 6:5). The result? Peace and prosperity — a democratic Utopia? No! "The earth also was corrupt before God and the earth was *filled* with violence .... *[A]ll* flesh had corrupted *his* way upon the earth" (verses 11 and 12).

The first experiment in democracy proved to be a total wash out — in more ways than one! All those who participated in the great experiment lost their lives in the Flood. The only ones spared were Noah, his wife, his three sons and their wives — a total of eight! (*Genesis* 7:1,11-24).

In case there are any readers who would scoff and hoot in derision at the biblical account of the Flood and Noah's Ark, we would point out that in recent years geologists — with the help of the most modern scientific equipment — have found, excavated, measured and photographed the remains of Noah's Ark exactly where your Bible said it "rested ... upon the mountain*s* [plural] of Ararat" (*Genesis* 8:4). The Bible did *not* say it landed on the Mountain of Ararat as many have assumed! (For further details, see *Discovered: Noah's Ark*, by Ron Wyatt).

While news of the discovery of the Ark has been ignored by "prestigious" Establishment publications such as *National Geographic*, the Turkish government has actually built a highway to the location of the Ark. The site is now a major tourist attraction.

BABYLON AND NIMROD

History records that, following the Flood, mankind lived under the laws of God and spoke one language. As the population expanded they began migrating from the area of the mountains of Ararat where the Ark landed (*Genesis* 8:4). "[A]s they journeyed from the east, they found a plain in the land of Shinar and dwelt there" (*Genesis* 11:1,2). [Shinar, a wonderfully fertile area, became the site of Babylon. Under Nimrod and his depraved wife, Semiramis, Babylon became the world capital of a God-rejecting, Satan-worshipping false religion. From Babylon and its religious system have come all the religious abominations that plague our world today.].

As was to be expected following the Flood, mankind as a whole refused to learn the lessons of history. Man slowly began to go back to seeking his own will — not that of his Creator! Predictably, the results were again catastrophic. Although the land continued to be marvelously productive, wild animals began to multiply at a faster rate than the rate of the people. They lived in terror of being attacked and consumed by these ferocious animals.

It was at this point that Nimrod came on the scene to exploit their fear. He became the "savior" of the terrified populace, organizing the people into walled towns and cities, where they would be protected from the wild animals. According to Hislop, Nimrod "became the object of high popularity.... The exploits of Nimrod ... gained for him the character of a great benefactor of his race....

"Had Nimrod gained renown only thus, it had been well. But not content with delivering man from the fear of the wild beasts, *he set to work to emancipate them from the fear of the Lord* which is the beginning of wisdom (*Proverbs* 9:10), and in which alone true happiness can be found. For this very thing he seems to have gained, as one of the titles by which men delighted to honor him, the title of 'Emancipator' or 'Deliverer'" (*The Two Babylons*, by Alexander Hislop, pp.50,51).

WHAT DO YOU MEAN BY "GOVERNMENT"?

In the final analysis the people didn't want to be independent, self-governing, and personally responsible for their own lives. In effect, they said, "Give us a king that he should rule over us; we will then be secure and free to do our own thing."

Observes Hislop: "*[M]en will readily rally around any man who can give the least appearance of plausibility to any doctrine that will teach them that they can be assured of happiness ... though their hearts and natures are unchanged, and though they live without God in the world.* [Nimrod] helped them put God and the strict spirituality of His law at a distance ... making men feel and act as if heaven were far away from earth, and as if the God of heaven 'could not see through the dark cloud,' or did not regard with displeasure the breakers of His law. Then all such would feel that they could breathe freely, and that now they could walk at liberty, *For this, such men could not but regard Nimrod as a high benefactor.*"

"THEY CHANGED THE TRUTH OF GOD"

In his rebellion against God — and in an effort to satisfy his inborn desire to worship — man "changed the truth of God into a lie and worshipped the creature [the creation or nature] rather than the Creator." As a result of refusing to "retain God in their knowledge [educational system], God gave them over to a reprobate mind" (*Romans* 1:25,28). While encouraging the worship of nature [the sun, the moon, "Mother Earth" (Gaia) etc], Nimrod set himself up as the priest of those things being worshipped by the people — thus gaining even more power and control over them.

Thus was born the Babylonian System of government. It is both civil and religious. People control is the name of that game!

We will deal more extensively with the Babylonian System in a later chapter.

ABRAHAM

It was into this rankly pagan, sun and moon-worshipping society that Abram (later Abraham) was born some years later. He was born in Ur of the Chaldees, the very center of idolatry.

It was from this sordid setting that the Creator God instructed Abraham to move out — on faith — and go to a land he would later be shown. He went! God made a covenant with Abraham, that through him all nations of the earth would be blessed. [This, of course, was fulfilled in Jesus Christ as is clearly shown in *Galatians* 5:16,28,29].

Later, Abraham had a son, Isaac, who, in turn, had a son named Jacob. Jacob, whose name was later changed to Israel, had twelve sons. With the passage of time, the families generated by the twelve sons became known as the twelve tribes of Israel.

Some 500 years later, following 460 years in Egypt and 40 years in the wilderness following the Exodus, the Creator God made a cast iron promise to the Hebrew people: "[I]f you will **obey** my voice indeed, and **keep** my covenant, **then** you shall be a peculiar people unto me above all people.... And you shall be unto me a kingdom of priests, *and a holy nation"* (*Exodus* 19:5). Note that it was conditional, "**if** you obey."

Later, having finally entered the Promised Land, after having been showered with awe-inspiring protection, that promise was repeated, only in much greater detail. In *Deuteronomy* 28:1-14 we read of the promise to the Hebrews that "**if** you shall hearken diligently unto the voice of the Lord your God, to observe and to **do all his** commandments, that the Lord your God **will** set you on high above all the nations of the earth.

"*And **all** these blessings **shall** come on you, **and overtake you,** if you shall hearken unto the voice of the Lord your God....*"

In the next verses, the Creator God reveals how he would richly bless them in every phase and facet of their lives **if** they would only trust and obey him. Then, in verses 15-68 God clearly lays out the **curses** that will come upon the Hebrews if they rebel and refuse to obey him.

The history of ancient Israel is particularly interesting in the way history repeats itself. Following Israel's entrance into the promised land (about 1425 B.C), "the people served the Lord *all the days of Joshua*, and *all* the days of the elders that outlived Joshua, who had *seen* all the great works of the Lord that he did for Israel" (*Judges* 2:7).

A few verses later we read that when "that generation were gathered to their fathers [or had died], *there arose another generation which knew not the Lord,* nor yet the works that he had done for Israel.

"And the children of Israel did evil in the sight of the Lord, and served Baalim [Satan the devil]."

WHAT DO YOU MEAN BY "GOVERNMENT"?

"And they forsook the Lord God of their fathers ... and followed other gods, the gods of the people that were around about them, and bowed themselves unto them, and provoked the Lord to anger.

"And they forsook the Lord, and served Baal and Ashtaroth" (vs.7,10,11,12,13).

In the years that ensued Israel had a checkered existence — with many ups and downs. God repeatedly raised up new leaders to help them return to sanity. However, when each such leader died the Israelites as a whole returned to their old ways. Periods of peace and prosperity were regularly followed by periods of war and deprivation. The people simply didn't want to obey God. Instead, they "corrupted themselves *more* than their fathers, in following other gods to serve them, and to bow down unto them; they ceased *not* from their *own* doings, nor from their *own* stubborn way" (v.19).

"GIVE US A KING"

As things got worse the leaders of the people came to Samuel, a judge and prophet in Israel. Their demand staggers the imagination. The people were no longer interested in having any kind of a personal relationship with their Creator God. They demanded Samuel to: "Give us a king to judge us *like all the nations*" (*1 Samuel* 8:5,6).

Scripture records that Samuel was greatly angered by their rebellious attitude. He went to God with his problem: "And the Lord said unto Samuel, Hearken unto the people ... *for they have not rejected you, but they have rejected me, that I should not reign over them*" (*v. 7*).

So that there would be no misunderstanding as to the ultimate outcome of such Satanically-inspired insanity, God told Samuel to "protest solemnly" to the people and show them what would happen as a result. The king would create a dictatorial regime; "he will take your fields and your vineyards, and your oliveyards, even the best of them, *and give them to his servants.*

"And he will take a tenth of your seed, and of your vineyards, and give them to his officers, and to his servants.

"And he will take your menservants, and your maidservants, and your goodliest young men, *and put them to his work....* and you shall be his servants.

"*And you shall cry out in that day because of your king which you shall have chosen you, and the Lord shall not hear you in that day*" (vs. 9-18).

Did the people recognize the error of their ways and withdraw their demand? No! They persisted in their wilful, stiffnecked, and strictly short-sighted rebellion against their Creator: *"[T]he people refused to obey the voice of Samuel; and they said, No; but we will have a king over us.*

"That we also may be like all the nations; and that our king may judge us, and go out before us, and fight our battles....

"And the Lord said to Samuel, Hearken unto their voice, and make them a king" (vs.20-22).

DOWNHILL

From that point on, with the possible exception of David and Solomon, the road was downhill all the way; the kingdom was divided in two (Israel and Judah). Later, both were conquered and went into captivity — Israel in 721 B.C., and Judah in 586 B.C.

Throughout the history of the Hebrew people only a remnant remained faithful to God; from them came Jesus Christ through whom came also spiritual redemption and salvation. As promised to Abraham, all nations of the world have been blessed in Christ (*Galatians* 3:16,26-29).

As predicted by Jesus Christ — and in perfect fulfillment of the terms of the agreement made by God with physical Israel — the covenantal relationship between God and the Hebrew race came to an end in 70 A.D. (*Matthew* 23:32-38). During the Roman siege of Jerusalem — in a final act of moral and spiritual depravity, the population of Jerusalem engaged in cannibalism as foretold in *Deuteronomy* 28:53.

This was the Great Tribulation prophesied by Jesus (*Matthew* 24:21). Those in Judea suffered 100 percent war casualties. Ninety percent were killed; the remaining ten percent were carried away captive to other nations. What greater tribulation could there be?

THE UNITED STATES COMPARED TO ANCIENT ISRAEL

In world history, the United States holds a unique position; it is the only nation since ancient Israel whose laws were based on the Word of God. From the time of the arrival of the Pilgrims the Bible was the

WHAT DO YOU MEAN BY "GOVERNMENT"? 17

basic law book. This was clearly laid out in the Mayflower Compact (signed November 20, 1620): "In the name of God, Amen. We whose names are underwritten ... for the glory of God, and advancement of the Christian faith ... covenant and combine ourselves together into a civil body politic, for our better ordering and preservation and furtherance of the ends aforesaid...."

A few years later John Winthrop, colonial governor of Connecticut, declared: "We shall be as a city on a hill. The eyes of all people are upon us; so if we shall deal falsely with our God in this work we have undertaken and so cause Him to withdraw His present help from us, we shall be made a story and a by-word through the world."

And John Madison, our fourth president, said: "We have staked the whole future of American civilization, *not* upon the power of government, *far from it*. We have staked the future ... upon the capacity of each and all of us to govern ourselves, to sustain ourselves, according to the Ten Commandments of God."

Finally, the testimony of Daniel Webster: *"[L]et us not forget the religious character of our origin. Our fathers were brought hither by their high veneration for the Christian religion. They journeyed by its light, and labored in its hope. They sought to incorporate its principles with the elements of their society."*

As documented in *Freedom or Slavery?* (Index D), by the present author and three co-authors, the Constitutions of all fifty states show that they are "Constitutionally Christian."

The U.S. Supreme Court (143 U.S. 457 at 471 [1892]; 343 U.S. 306 at 313 [1952], and 366 U.S. 420 at 461 [1961]) has ruled that this is a Christian Nation.

As such, the United States prospered as no other nation in history; we were in a league by ourselves. "Aflame with righteousness" (de Tocqueville), and diligent in our application of the laws and principles found in scripture, God "set us above all the nations of the earth.... Blessings overtook us." We appeared invulnerable.

BUT.... The comparison between the U.S. and ancient Israel is staggering. Like them, "we forsook the God of our fathers ... and followed other gods, the gods of the people round about us, and bowed down to them."

With the passage of time, also like them, we "corrupted ourselves *more* than our fathers, in following other gods to serve them; we ceased not from our own doings, nor from our own stubborn way."

Throughout all history human nature has been a constant!

"GIVE US A KING"

Unknown by most, our Christian Republic (with individual self-government and personal responsibility under God) came to an end in 1933 with the arrival of Franklin D. Roosevelt and his humanistic/-socialistic/democratic (the State is god) philosophy. Like Nimrod of old, Roosevelt appeared as a "Deliverer" or "Emancipator."

At that fateful time, the American people (like the ancient Israelites before them) said in effect: "We're tired of being self-governing and personally responsible for our actions. *Give us a king to judge us ... like all the other nations.*" God has not forsaken America. America has wilfully forsaken God!

Again following the pattern of old, our national fate is becoming virtually identical to that of ancient Israel. Our new god is "the state" and he has turned into a fearful, rampaging master. The state god is a "jealous god" — one which tries desperately to emulate the true God by adopting the First Commandment, "You shall have no other gods before me."

Over the last 60 plus years America's jealous god has displayed an ever-growing proclivity to steal, murder, and destroy in order to impose its will. Using deceit, coercion, harassment, pressure and intimidation, the state god has virtually taxed the nation to death; it has stolen our land, and turned us into slaves. "He has erected a multitude of New Offices, and sent hither swarms of Officers to harass our people, and eat out [our] substance...." (*Declaration of Independence*). In addition, the state god has built up a debt of nearly $6 Trillion — or $15,000 plus for every man, woman and child in the land. Also, through its support of abortion, the state god has sacrificed some 30,000,000 American children to Satan since 1973.

MIGHT AND INGENUITY

In his Satanically-inspired rebellion against his Creator, man has striven with all his might and ingenuity to figure out a way around God's existence and sovereignty. He adamantly refuses to accept the fact that — by his own efforts — he is totally incapable of achieving true peace and prosperity. Hope dwells eternal in the carnal mind! Now, as we approach the beginning of another millennium, he believes he finally has it all figured out: the creation of a New World Order super state.

We must recognize that the state god is inspired in its ambitions by Satan, "the father of lies" and the "god of this world" (*II Corinthians* 4:4) — the one who "deceives the whole world" (*Revelation* 12:9). Satan is the one who deceives man into believing he can be "as god" and create his own utopia!

THE ULTIMATE QUESTION

The ultimate question is, of course, **Who's the boss?** Once you settle and establish that the Creator God is Sovereign, that Jesus Christ is Lord, and that the Bible is the inerrant word of God, 90% of your troubles are over. *You know who gives the orders!*

Jesus Christ is **The Way, The Truth, and The Life**. At the name of Jesus every knee shall bow ... and every tongue confess that Jesus Christ is Lord to the glory of God the father.

In Adam all die, even so in Christ shall all be made alive (I Corinthians 15:22).

Let God be true and every man a liar! (*Romans* 3:4).

Chapter 4

WHAT IS MAN?

In today's society we are confronted with glaring contrasts — contrasts which can, alternately, inspire flights of euphoria or plunge us into depths of despair.

In the physical world we are surrounded by the awesome splendor of God's creation with its myriad manifestations of design, beauty, harmony and lawfulness; we also marvel at the almost unbelievable inventions that have exploded and proliferated on the world scene particularly over the last 200 years. The laws, principles and materials built into nature by a loving Creator God have enabled us to discover or uncover principles which, when understood and developed, have enabled us to make our lives much more comfortable and productive. Electrical power, radios, phones, automobiles, refrigerators, air conditioning, planes, television, fax machines and modems are just a few such discoveries.

It is vitally important, however, that we clearly recognize the fact that these and many additional marvels of "modern technology" were not — in the truest sense of the word — invented or created by man. The laws, principles and materials involved in their creation and development were merely discovered by man. The technology

WHAT IS MAN?

involved was developed by many thousands, perhaps millions, of individuals working on the basis of what had previously been uncovered. "There is nothing new under heaven."

Individually, we should rejoice in the benefits these discoveries bring to our lives — and then use them to the fullest possible advantage in helping all of mankind to develop still further.

A PROBLEM

But there is a problem — a **major** problem! In spite of all mankind's wonderful physical or technological advances most people are living lives that sadly fail to reflect any significant growth or development of skills in dealing with their fellow human beings. It would probably be true to say that such relationships have, in fact, degenerated significantly in recent times.

Despite the massive proliferation of "experts" in the field of human relations, there has been no accompanying proliferation in the understanding of and solutions to human problems. Why? Could it be that psychiatrists and psychologists insist on dealing with the symptoms of the problem instead of actually dealing with the problem itself? Could it also be that the problem is not just psychological (or mental) in nature, but rather *spiritual*?

When we examine the histories of bygone civilizations, and then compare our findings with what we see around us in today's allegedly advanced and proudly "sophisticated" society, one is tempted to hang one's head in despair. It seems that our much-ballyhooed and loudly-trumpeted high-tech society hasn't learned a single one of the lessons written in the blood, toil, tears, and sweat of civilizations past. The historical lessons — both political and religious — preserved from the time of the ancient Egyptians, Assyrians, Babylonians, Hebrews, Greeks, and the Romans have not just been overlooked; they have been deeply buried under millions of tons of modern political, social and religious garbage — by both the secular and ecclesiastical authorities. Working in tandem, these forces have succeeded in clouding the issues and in making our people amazingly unaware of what is actually happening on the national and international scenes.

It is extremely interesting that so many so-called Americans should pride themselves on their "sophistication." Noah Webster's *American Dictionary of the English Language* (1828) defines sophistication as: "The act of adulteration; a counterfeiting or debasing the purity of something by a foreign admixture; adulteration." Webster further defines a sophist is, "A captious or fallacious reasoner."

Could it be that the sophisticated "experts" are in fact wrong, and are thus operating off a false premise — a "previous proposition from which another follows as a conclusion"? Could it also be true that such a premise, based on captious or fallacious reasoning, could have led to our present social crisis of monumental proportions?

In the final analysis, we must realize that the decisions we make are only as good as the information (premises) upon which they are based. If we start off with a false premise or assumption, *everything* built thereon will be structurally unsound — and will thus ultimately come to nothing!

If we are to make significant progress in unravelling the mysteries of life itself, we must first understand the nature of the problem, and why things are the way they are.

"WHAT"S IT ALL ABOUT, ALFIE?"

"What's it all about, Alfie?" This question, posed in the words of a popular song of some years ago, reflects a nagging question that has haunted the psyches of every thinking person since the dawn of time.

To most, their existence is a riddle wrapped up in an enigma. Few if any of the people or organizations we have come to accept as "authorities" have even remotely come close to providing answers to this most basic of human dilemmas.

What are we? Who are we? Why are we here? Where did we come from? Were we in fact created, or are we just the result of a cosmic accident? Where are we headed? Is there any purpose to our all-too-often mundane existence? Yes, what's it all about, Alfie?

These are *the* basic questions of life. They must be addressed before we can make any significant progress in our quest to unravel the mysteries of life.

Basic truth and understanding are of vital importance. From the outset we must recognize the fact that when we initiate a search based upon a false premise *everything* built upon that erroneous foundation will be out of sync with basic reality. The more we build upon that basic false premise the further we get away from true stability.

False premises lie at the heart and core of modern society's monumental problems. Especially over the last hundred years, our great institutions (education, religion, banking, family etc.) have been restructured and rebuilt upon premises that are at total variance with the foundational principles which guided our Founding Fathers. The results were historically predictable. As these institutions developed they became increasingly unsound structurally. Their untenable foundations are now cracking, crumbling and falling apart at the seams. Being built on the quicksand of wishful humanistic (man is god) thinking and in violation of the laws and principles laid down by God, they just can't stand up under the pressures of the real world. It is inevitable that they will all collapse in ignominious piles of worthless, irredeemable garbage.

HOW ABOUT YOU?

How about **you**? How sound are your foundations? Are they imbedded in rock ... or are they also collapsing in the midst of the ever shifting sands of time? Are you floundering — without a rudder or anchor — in the tumultuous, storm-tossed ocean of life? In despair, do you feel like giving up your efforts to find a purpose in life? Yes, "What's it all about, Alfie?"

To find the answer to that most basic of questions, we must start with the lowest common denominator, the most basic ingredient of human society — the human individual. Unless and until we understand the who, what, and why of the human individual — the basic building block from which all human society is built — we can make no significant progress. Without this basic knowledge and understanding we can't even begin to take our first, faltering steps towards acquiring true understanding — and the answers we allegedly seek.

What is life all about? When we consult the "experts" and famed philosophers in search of the answer we get almost as many "answers" as there are experts to expound them. When we attempt to analyze the expert evidence presented, we end up more confused and frustrated than when we first began our questioning process. To say that confusion reigns in this area of knowledge and understanding of humankind is to couch the truth in the mildest possible terms.

WHAT IS MAN?

What is man? Is there any sure way to tell? Humanly speaking, no! Your opinion is as good as mine, **worthless**! To debate the subject is both time consuming and frustrating. It inevitably degenerates into a profitless exchange of "mythinformation," vain philosophy, and mindless speculation. Mankind's opinions are a waste of time. No worthwhile purpose is served. They are an exercise in futility.

WHEN ALL ELSE FAILS...

Is there any other source through which we may be able to accurately acquire this most crucial of all basic information? A clue to the whereabouts of such a source comes from a sign posted on the word processor upon which this chapter was originally typed: It simply states, "When all else fails, read the instructions."

When man showed up on planet earth, did an instruction manual come as part of the package? Did his "manufacturer" send along some instructions to show what makes man tick? Was the basic product defective? Did the manufacturer make a hideous mistake? Should a recall notice have been issued almost immediately?

The ultra-sophisticated (those with "captious and fallacious reasoning" — Webster) will deride such "moronic" questions as these; to give them credence would be beneath their lofty dignity!

But Stop and Think! When we consider the grim plight in which mankind currently finds itself, it is obvious that something is terribly wrong. Could we be overlooking or choosing to ignore some very basic knowledge that could make all the difference in our understanding of life itself?

There is only one book in existence that some consider to be the missing operator's manual of the human race, the book that supplies us with the information necessary to answer the basic question, "What's life all about?"

That book, of course, is the Bible. Some churchgoers still believe it to be the inerrant instruction manual of the Creator (Manufacturer) God, but most don't! That's at least part of the problem!

On the wild off-chance that this "archaic," much maligned source might possibly contain the answer to the question, "What is man?" let's take a look at what it has to say.

The Bible declares that, "In the beginning God made the heaven and the earth" (*Genesis* 1:1). And "God created man in his own image, in the image of God created he him; male and female created he them" (*Genesis* 1:27). Like everything else in God's creation, man was "very good" (v.31). In fact, man was created only "a little lower than the angels" (*Psalm* 8:5). Being God's ultimate physical creation, man was also the crowning jewel of that creation. As such, he was "given

WHAT IS MAN?

dominion over ... every living thing that move[d] upon the earth" (v.28).

Shortly after Adam's creation God formed the first woman, Eve, from one of Adam's ribs as he was in a deep sleep (*Genesis* 2:21-23). They then became man and wife. In verse 25 we read that they "were both naked, the man and his wife, and were *not* ashamed." That last statement is of crucial importance. In their natural, God-created environment and when they were living in accordance with his laws, they had no feelings of inadequacy, inferiority, or of not "having it all together." They were at peace with themselves and with their Creator as they followed **His** instructions to "Be fruitful, and multiply, and replenish the earth, and subdue it and have dominion over the fish of the sea, and over the fowl of the air, and everything that moveth upon the earth" (*Genesis* 1:28).[1]

THE SERPENT

In *Genesis* 3:1, however, we read of the arrival on the scene of "the serpent" who is described as being "more subtil than any beast of the field which the Lord God had made." Elsewhere this personality is identified as "that old serpent, called the Devil and Satan, which deceives the whole world" (*Revelation* 12:9). Where he originated is explained in chapter 5.

Notice the tactics the serpent employed in his confrontation with Eve. He twisted and questioned the clear instructions that God had previously given her husband (*Genesis* 2:16,17): "Of every tree of the garden you may freely eat.

"But of the tree of the knowledge of good and evil, you shall not eat of it: for in the day that you eat thereof you shall surely die." The serpent challenged the veracity of God's word. He jeeringly said, "Yes, has God said, You shall not eat of every tree of the garden." Notice the twist? He basically reversed God's instructions.

Eve was clearly aware of the instructions given by her Maker as she repeated *most* of them in *Genesis* 3:2,3. However, not quite content with God's word, Eve added her own unique twist. She distorted

---

[1] In theological terms, man is a combination of body, soul, and spirit. The body consists of the physical, feeling part; the soul is the life force, and seat of the emotions, and the spirit is the seat of the intellect.

God's word by quoting God as having said regarding the "tree which in the midst of the garden": "You shall not eat of it, **neither shall you touch it**, lest you die." God never said not to touch it! In fact God specifically ordered Adam "to dress it and keep it." That most certainly involves "touching it."

Next, the serpent appealed to Eve's human nature, her pride, vanity and ego. In essence he declared that God was a liar, a deceiver — one who wants to withhold that which is good and right from people. The serpent told Eve that when she and her husband obeyed *his* instructions to eat of the forbidden tree they would then become "as gods knowing good and evil."

The serpent's pitch had Eve drooling at the mouth. He played her like a master violinist would his instrument, zeroing in on all the weaknesses of her human nature — her pride and vanity, her lust and greed. Eve bought into the serpent's deadly bait; in fact she swallowed it hook, line, and sinker! She and then her husband consciously chose to accept the strictly intangible short-term "blessings" promised by the serpent over of the long-term tangible blessings guaranteed by God.

Notice verse 6: "And when the woman *saw* that the [forbidden] tree was good for food, and that it was *pleasant to the eye*, and a tree *desired* to make one wise, she took of the fruit thereof and did eat, *and gave also unto her husband with her; and he did eat.*"

[It is probable that this particular "fruit" contained a substance which changed their molecular structure (body chemistry) and thus created conditions which automatically led to physical death. "In Adam all die...." (*I Corinthians* 15:22)].

Grasp the last part of verse 6. Adam was with Eve during all this time. Although he was not deceived like Eve (*I Timothy* 2:14), Adam relinquished his God-given role as husband and leader, went along for the ride, and participated in his wife's folly. He rebelled and sinned against his Creator. The consequences are laid out in *Genesis* 3:14-24).

What was Adam's reaction after he and his wife rebelled? Did he immediately acknowledge his sin and repent? Was he deeply broken up over his disobedience? The astounding answer to that question is also found in *Genesis 3*. A drastic change had occurred. For the first time in his life Adam realized he and his wife were naked. They became afraid and tried to hide from God by sewing together fig leaves and wearing them as aprons (vs.7-10). They tried to cover up their sin rather than repent. When the cover-up didn't work, then the buck was passed.

When confronted by his Creator over his disobedience, Adam did something that has been copied by his descendants down through the eons of time — he passed the buck! Read it with your own eyes in verse 12. It's a mind blower: "And the man said, The woman whom **you** gave to be with me, **she** gave me of the tree and I did eat." In other words, Adam said: "God, **you** are to blame for all our troubles! **You** are responsible for screwing up our lives!"

Things haven't really changed over the years since, have they? Men and woman are still passing the buck. They are still making excuses. They are still denying reality. And they are still trying to hide their nakedness before God behind their "fig leaves" which come in all shapes and sizes. Human nature is a constant — it never changes!

CYCLE OF FAILURE
AND DESTRUCTION

At this juncture we need to understand what could be called the Cycle of Failure and Destruction; it could, more correctly perhaps, be called the not-so-merry-go-round of the human experience.

As we all go through life, we experience numerous trials and tests. How these are handled will determine the quality of our lives.

When most people are faced with difficulties or problems, they feel pressure or anxiety. In all too many cases the way in which they react leads to failure and even more anxiety. Failure breeds fear and in most cases this leads to some form of compensation. The latter can take many forms — reaching for a cigarette or a drink, buying new clothes they don't really need, going to a movie, taking a trip, going out to dinner, joining a club ... anything to take their minds off the problem and their inability to adequately cope with it. This inevitably leads to more pressure, more failure, and a repetition of the cycle.

Stop and think! How many times have you found yourself on such a cycle? Hundreds? Thousands?

For the vast majority, the cycle of (1) Problem, (2) Pressure, (3) Reaction, (4) Failure, and (5) Compensation is repeated with monotonous regularity. As a result life is a never-ending, soul-destroying grind for most. Until the cycle is analyzed, understood, and correctly addressed there is no hope of truly significant progress — and ultimate victory over it.

Recognizing and understanding our own physical, mental and psychological makeups — and then calmly facing reality — will go a long way toward solving most problems.

FACING REALITY ABOUT OURSELVES

It's time to realize the startling accuracy of what you have just read from the pages of your own Bible. Hopefully, your new found knowledge and understanding, gained from the word of God, will be instrumental in opening up still further areas of knowledge and discernment. But first, we must learn to face some plain, simple, basic truths about ourselves — personally and individually.

In *Genesis* 2:7, in the first biblical reference to humankind, we read that "God formed man of the dust of the ground..."

Precisely, what does that verse say? If we are to be absolutely honest, we must not add anything to that verse, nor must we take anything from it. Without any embellishment, *Genesis* 2:7 clearly tells us that, physically speaking, we are just plain dirt. Nothing more; nothing less. In the vernacular, our Manufacturer is telling us that we are all "clods" of dirt. This is basic, foundational knowledge.

If, in a burst of intellectual vanity or spiritual pride, we stamp our feet in anger and choose to reject this basic statement of fact, it must be clearly understood that we are engaged in human speculation. We no longer believe our Maker, and are thus no longer dealing in the realm of reality. If we, personally and individually, insist upon building our lives upon such a false foundation or premise, we must realize that any and all attempts to solve our personal problems will, of necessity, end in failure.

Everything we build upon our humanly devised new premise must, by its very nature, be false. It won't be founded upon a rock, an immovable foundation. It won't stand up to close scrutiny, and will inevitably crumble when put to the acid test. It's doomed to failure!

With this basic reality firmly in mind, fellow clods, let us proceed.

MAN'S HEART

In His instruction manual, what does man's Manufacturer reveal about man's "heart" and natural proclivities — the way man **is** (as opposed to the way in which he would **like to be** perceived)?

WHAT IS MAN?

This humanly obnoxious and ego-shattering revelation is found in *Jeremiah* 17:9: "The heart of man is *deceitful* above *all* things, and *desperately wicked*: who can know it?"

Who, indeed, can know it? Our hearts (our natural innermost thoughts, goals and aspirations) are so *deceitful* and *desperately wicked* that none of us, naturally speaking, want to recognize and openly acknowledge the awful truth about ourselves. To avoid a face-to-face confrontation with reality and an acknowledgment of the truth, we play the most bizarre games and indulge in the most extreme forms of mental gymnastics. We will virtually do *anything* (even pay exorbitant sums to psychiatrists and psychologists) in a desperate effort to avoid such a hideously horrifying confrontation with truth!

THE CARNAL MIND

Let's go still further, fellow clods, "deceitful above all things" members of the human race. How about our minds?[2] Are they any improvement over our hearts?

Our Maker settles that question in *Romans* 8:7: "[T]he *carnal mind* [the natural, *fleshy, meaty* mind with which we are all born] is *enmity against God*: for it is *not* subject to the law of God, *neither indeed can be.*"

This is our Manufacturer's blunt, no-holds-barred revelation regarding His creation. *He calls us all 'meatheads.'* That is the way we are, naturally speaking! Could anything be clearer or more brutally frank? Hardly!

To admit our true condition would be to confess the fact that our whole life has been a massive charade. Our adamant, carnal minded refusal to make such a confession results in a carefully orchestrated, meticulously cultivated, and monstrously hypocritical lifestyle. Every word, every action is specifically designed to deceive others and to project a favorable "image" of ourselves to the world. Like every image, it is the exact opposite to reality. For example, when you look at your image in a mirror everything is reversed. In the mirror image, your right hand is the image's left hand, your left eye is the image's right eye. In addition, there is no substance to the image.

---

[2] Sometimes the words "heart" and "mind" mean the same thing: "[A]s he thinks in his heart, so is he...." (*Proverbs* 23:7).

The image we present to the world is, of course, carefully molded through the deceitfulness of our hearts; it is designed to make us *look* good, so that we can *feel* good about ourselves. However, deep down in our innermost being, we have no thought or interest in *being* good. Tragically, we soon begin to believe our own lies.

"O what a tangled web we weave when we practice to deceive."

All our eloquent protestations to the contrary are just so much pious cant. This, too, is calculated to deceive!

To acknowledge the truth and act upon it would be tantamount to committing social suicide — a horrifyingly ghastly possibility that must be avoided at all costs!

I mean, "what would people think" if we were to admit our truly miserable and wretched condition? Our perceived reputation as "one of the pillars of the local community" would be totally shattered. We would be "looked down on" by those whose pharisaic and lying opinions we value. Our "standing" in the community would be destroyed! That, alone, is an appalling thought!

In the final analysis, our lives are nothing more than hollow monuments to hypocritical futility; erected upon a series of false premises that have long-since been buried under mountains of deception. Our lives are nothing more than pompous balloons filled with fantasy and make-believe. There is nothing inside but hot air!

We were conned into believing the Satanic lie that we would be "as gods" (*Genesis* 3:7), but now we are scared to admit our error.

Our "lifestyles" (all our posing, posturing, and frantic efforts to be well thought of by others) are nothing more than *deathstyles*. They are destroying us. But we are too proud and self-righteous to admit the hideous truth — **and change**.

That's the way we **are**. No ifs, no buts, no maybes, no possiblys!

FACING THE TRUTH

Will we squarely face the truth? Will we admit the reality of our truly frightful condition? Until we do, we can't even begin to take our first, faltering steps towards the full, joyful, abundant life we all desire. Like Carnation, the world may have an abundance of "contented cows" but it has precious few contented people!

In the Manufacturer's Handbook another critical statement of fact appears; it is, however, for one reason or another, generally ignored or totally misunderstood by those who feel led to expound the Word!

In *Matthew* 9:16-17 Jesus Christ states: "No man puts a piece of new cloth unto an old garment, for that which is put in to fill it up takes from the garment and the tear is made worse.

"Neither do men put new wine into old bottles; else the bottles break, and the wine runs out, and the bottles perish: but they put new wine into new bottles, and both are preserved."

Read those words from Matthew 9:13-17 again — slowly and carefully! Ponder their vital significance! Jesus is speaking about those "sinners [who would come] to repentance" (v.13). He is speaking of those who would come to Him for both Redemption and Salvation.

Jesus is saying that when people are called by God's Sovereign Grace to repentance it would be extremely foolish for them to assume that they can satisfactorily build their new lives "in Christ" on their old foundation of humanism that had proved so untrustworthy in the past.

No! To live truly successful Christian lives each of us must, after our calling and conversion, go back to square one. We must start over. We must be willing to jettison all the mental, philosophical and religious flotsam and jetsam we have so mindlessly accumulated since birth. *Everything must go.* There is no other way. Everything else has been tried. Everything else has failed! In Christ "all things [including the foundation of our lives] become new" (*II Corinthians* 5:17).

SAVING YOUR "LIFE"

Another critical piece of Biblical understanding is revealed in *Mark* 8:35: "For whosoever will save his life *shall* lose it; but whosoever shall lose his life for my sake and the gospel's, the same shall save it."

This truth appears a total of three times in your Bible (*Matthew* 16:25, *Mark* 8:35, and *Luke* 9:24). But what does it really mean? What is this "life" one has to lose in order to find the true life which is in Christ (*John* 14:6)?

Simple! We have to get rid of (lose!) all of the lies, falsehoods, mental games, charades, deceitfulness, and excuses in which all humans indulge in a desperate attempt to escape from the excruciating reality of what they truly are. We must see, acknowledge, understand, and repent of — and turn away from — all those things that are part of the human "coping mechanism" which strives to gloss over or cover up most of the monumental shortcomings, fears, doubts and inadequacies which plague people from the cradle to the grave. Although all these things have the appearance of making life more tolerable for most people, *they are in fact diabolically destructive forms of artificial respiration.* They don't symbolize life; they represent death. As scripture clearly states, those who strive to save their own phony, ego-protecting, artificial "life," will lose it; but whosoever shall lose (repent of and jettison) their phony, counterfeit, never-satisfied life for Christ's sake shall, in fact, save it."

Because they stand in the way of the "abundant life" promised to us through Jesus Christ (*John* 10:10), the fraudulent, artificial "lives" we live must be acknowledged and repented of. Jesus Christ, alone, is the way, the truth and the life (*John* 14:6).

The genuine spiritual *life* that true Christians receive in and through Jesus is totally supernatural; it leads to "the peace of God that passes understanding." Being void of any artificiality, it "shall keep our hearts and minds through [the life of] Jesus Christ" (*Philippians* 4:7). It is the risen, living Lord Jesus Christ who saves **His** people from their sins (*Matthew* 1:21).

"He that believeth on me, as the scripture has said, out of his belly [innermost being] shall flow rivers of living water" (*John* 7:38). When that happens to an individual, there will be no time for phoniness, lies, deceit, and game playing.

"Therefore **if** any man be in Christ, he is a new creature: old things are passed away; behold, all things are become new" (*II Corinthians* 5:17). They will no longer feel any need for artificial respiration. They will have **the real thing!**

Through the power of the Holy Spirit (the spirit of "power, and of love, and of a sound mind" — *II Timothy* 1:7), which, spiritually speaking, operates somewhat like a radar scanner, we must freely and openly examine each and every one of our basic premises and preconceived ideas to ensure that every aspect of our lives is in accord with reality. The living word of God is "quick and powerful, and sharper than any two-edged sword, piercing even to the dividing asunder of soul and spirit, and of the joints and marrow, and is a discerner of the thoughts and intents of the heart" (*Hebrews* 4:12).

If we will only get out of the way, the word of God will cut through all the charades and deceitfulness of our human reasoning and lay bare the true thoughts and intents of our hearts. It will dig up and lay bare all the false premises and misconceptions we have accumulated since birth — those ideas which have resulted in repeated failures in every phase and facet of our lives (v.13).

Only then can we truly "grow in grace, and in the knowledge of our Lord and Savior Jesus Christ. To him be glory both now and for ever. Amen" (*II Peter* 3:18).

Chapter 5

SATAN'S PLAN: A MASTERPIECE OF DIABOLICAL INGENUITY

It should be abundantly clear to any objective person viewing the world of the late twentieth century that mankind is in deep trouble; something is desperately wrong! When the unregenerate minds of society's experts express opinions as to the cause of mankind's predicament they come up with a wide variety of glib theories. Their hypotheses, however, have one common problem — they are all based on human speculation, assumptions, and a lack of knowledge and understanding. In the end, however, their hypotheses are all revealed as vain efforts to explain the otherwise inexplicable. As one guess is as good or bad as another, they end up going around in circles getting nowhere — and thus fail to explain the condition in which we find ourselves. While knowledge and understanding in so many areas expands at a rapid pace, no such progress is evident in the area of reversing the mess in which mankind finds itself.

As a result, the crisis deepens. Around the globe, billions — swept to and fro on tidal waves of deception and contradictory speculations

— are sinking ever deeper into personal quagmires of frustration and anguish. Most — having given up hope — exist in a state of despair.

THE SOURCE OF TRUE KNOWLEDGE AND UNDERSTANDING

There is one source that claims to have all the answers to the questions and dilemmas outlined above: the Bible. Interestingly enough, although countless millions around the world profess to believe that the Bible is God's word and revelation to mankind, all too few exhibit a genuine interest in understanding its message and incorporating its truths in their everyday lives.

God's word is crystal clear as to the causes of society's ills. Before going into the biblical background of evil and corruption, however, we need to note the fact that the New Testament reveals the existence of a personality described as "the prince of the power of the air" (*Ephesians* 2:2). Jesus Christ identifies this entity as being a powerful angelic being named Satan (*Luke* 10:18); he acknowledged that Satan is the Prince of Devils (*Matthew* 12:24-27; *Mark* 3:22—26); Jesus also called him "the prince of this world" (*John* 12:31). Elsewhere, this personality is identified as, the "Devil and Satan who has deceived the whole world" (*Revelation* 12:9). Further, it is revealed that Satan is able to transform or change himself so as to appear as "an angel of light" (*II Corinthians* 11:14). Not only that, but the great deceiver has his own ministers: "Therefore it is no great thing if his ministers also be transformed **as** the ministers of righteousness...." (v.15).

All the uncalled, unconverted, unsaved people of this world "walk according to the course of this world, according to the prince of the power of the air, the spirit that now works in the children of disobedience" (*Ephesians* 2:2).

In other words, Satan has laid out a course or "way" in which he wants people to walk; *it's his way!* To fallen man, that "way" — one rooted in jealousy, vanity, lust and greed — seems so right, so normal; it is so addictive that he is astonished that anyone would have the audacity to suggest that it might not be the path upon which one should travel through life. That way, however, leads to everything that is destructive; it ultimately ends in death (*Proverbs* 16:25).

Satan has in fact designed a wide variety of "ways." Each one is tailored to suit various types and personalities of individuals all across the social, political and religious spectrum. He can thus deceive, lead, manipulate, and control most of the populace into going along with his system of government on planet Earth.

WHERE DID SATAN COME FROM?

But stop! Where did Satan come from? Obviously, he didn't just suddenly appear accidentally on the world scene. Where did he originate? How did he end up in opposition to the Creator God? But now that he has done so, what are his plans for the future? And, most important of all, will those plans be brought to fruition?

Again, we must go to our Maker's manual in search of answers.

In the Bible we read that, "In the beginning, God created the heaven and the earth.... And God saw everything that he had made, and, behold, it was very good (*Genesis* 1:1,31). "Thus the heavens and the earth were finished and all the *host* of them" (*Genesis* 2:1). The word "host" indicates that the angels were included in the creation, and that they were "very good."

But something of far-reaching importance happened for, in the third chapter, verse 1, we read of the appearance of the Serpent — later identified as "the Devil and Satan" (*Revelation* 12:9). What happened between creation and the time Eve and the Serpent had their fateful meeting? The answer to that question is revealed later in the Bible — in *Isaiah* 14 and *Ezekiel* 28. These passages reveal that at the time of creation God had placed Lucifer, an archangel who "sealed up the sum, full of wisdom and perfect in beauty," over the angelic host (*Ezekiel* 28:12,14,15). Lucifer was "perfect in [his] ways" when he was created (v.15).

The name Lucifer means "son of the morning," "the shining one," or "shining star [or angel, see *Revelation* 1:20] of the dawn." As the Light Bringer, Lucifer was the "covering cherub," the archangel whom God had placed over the other angels and whose outspread wings literally covered the very throne of God. As the Creator had placed him in charge of all other angels, Lucifer obviously had awesome power and authority. He was, in fact, #2 only to God himself!

A REAL ATTITUDE PROBLEM

But Lucifer soon developed a real attitude problem. He wasn't satisfied with what his Creator had given him; he wanted more power. Consumed with jealousy, vanity, lust and greed, he conceived a

SATAN'S PLAN

grandiose plan to become #1 — the Big Boss! In other words, he wanted to kick the Creator God off his throne and take over the universe! How's that for ambition?

The truth about Lucifer's massive powerplay is revealed in the fourteenth chapter of *Isaiah*. Beginning in verse 4, we see the king of Babylon pictured as a raging tyrant who was a curse to his subjects. No wonder! Scripture shows clearly that he was a tool of his master, Satan. He was being used as a pawn in Satan's game plan.

This fact becomes clear when we read verses 12-14. Here, the lesser type lifts to the great antitype — Satan — who controlled him. The reader will notice that things are said in these verses that could not be said about a mere human being; they lay bare what happened in heaven sometime after creation: "How are you fallen from heaven, O Lucifer, son of the morning. How are you cut down to the ground, who did weaken the nations?

"For you have said in your heart, I will ascend into [or, IN] heaven [the location of God's throne], I will exalt my throne about the stars [angels, *Revelation* 1:20] of God; I will sit also upon the mountain of the congregation, in the sides of the north.

"I [notice the big "I" again!] will ascend above the heights of the clouds; I will be like the Most High.

"Yet you shall be brought down to hell, to the sides of the pit."

Another graphic account of Lucifer's rebellion against his Creator is found in *Ezekiel* 28. Although this is again addressed to a man, the king of Tyrus, it is obviously aimed at the power behind the throne — Lucifer: "You seal up the sum, full of wisdom, and perfect in beauty (verse 12).

"You have been in Eden the Garden of God" (v.13).

"You are the anointed cherub that covers; and I have set you so.... (v.14).

"You were perfect in your ways from the day that you were created, till iniquity was found in you.... (v.15).

"Your heart was lifted up because of your beauty, you have corrupted your wisdom by reason of your brightness: I will cast you to the ground, I will lay you before kings, that they may see you.

"You have defiled your sanctuaries by the multitude of your iniquities...."

This obviously could not have been said of the literal, physical prince of Tyre. God is clearly addressing Satan, "the prince of the power of the air, the spirit that now works in the children of disobedience (*Ephesians* 2:2).

As a result of his insubordination, God condemned Lucifer: "I will cast you as profane out of the mountain of God ... [since] your heart is lifted up because of your beauty, you have corrupted your wisdom by reason of your brightness.... You have defiled your sanctuaries by the multitude of your iniquities, by the iniquity of your traffick" (*Ezekiel* 28:16,17,18).

One-third of the angels followed Satan in his rebellion (*Revelation* 12:4;1:20). As a result, they became demons. Satan and his demons now rule the world scene through a hierarchial system of "principalities" and "powers"; these are the "rulers of the darkness of this world ... spiritual wickedness [or wicked spirits] in high places" (*Ephesians* 6:12).

For additional details on Satan's modus operandi, we conclude this section of the book with segments from an article entitled "The Plan of Satan in the Plain of Shinar," written by Pastor Conrad Jarrell, III. It appeared in the May/June, 1989, issue of *Midnight Messenger*, and is used with his kind permission:

THE FORCES THAT SHAPE HISTORY

The Bible has a great deal to say about the world and the forces that shape its history. Being the revelation of the Creator, its value in this area is immense. If there are forces at work more powerful than humans alone, then it follows that those forces must be dominant in world history. The Bible asserts the existence of such forces. In fact, it goes far beyond asserting — the forces are identified, described, and defined. Most interesting of all, the plan and method of these forces shaping world history are described in detail.

Now, this is pretty heady stuff to say about one person, even if he is an angel. But then, the Bible indicates that there are some very powerful angels. In the book of *Daniel*, mighty angels are referred to as princes of such nations as Persia, Grecia, and Israel (*Daniel* 10:13,20-21). It would seem that the ultimate rulers of the world's nations are not human at all, but are angelic.

ANGELIC PRINCES

Put it all together. The nations of this world are ruled ultimately by angelic beings, called *Princes* of those nations. These angelic Princes

SATAN'S PLAN

— except Michael, the Prince of Israel — and all other angels allied with them, are ruled by the Prince of Devils, Satan, who is also the Prince of this world. The course of the world — the way, the path, the channel of movement of its events — is according to his power. Finally, the whole world is deceived by Satan concerning both this fact and his methods.

I emphasize: **If** there is a Creator God, and **if** the Bible is His revelation to Mankind, **then**... *this is the way things really are.* And anyone — anyone at all — who denies the above conclusions, must of necessity be deceived by Satan, the Prince of This World. Of course, the public educators, the news media, almost all scientists, most religious leaders, and the government officials of the world's nations all deny this state of affairs. But then, this is to be expected, isn't it?

So then — the course of world history moves according to the power of Satan and his angelic princes. But, according to what plan? Toward what end? How?

SATAN'S WORLD SYSTEM

Now, we have come up against a brick wall. One of the recurrent metaphors in the Bible for Satan's World System is The Strange Woman, usually depicted as a harlot who fornicates with the nations of the earth (see especially *Revelation* 17:1—5,18). An extremely important fact is revealed about this World System in *Proverbs* 5:3, 6: "For the lips of **a strange woman** drop as an honeycomb, and her mouth is smoother than oil.... Lest you should ponder the path of life, **her ways are moveable, that you can not know them.**" If Satan "deceives the *whole* world," and if his System's "ways are changeable so that you *can not* know them," then we come to a brick wall: There is no way to figure out The System *from within The System!* For, alas! Everything in the world **is** The System. Except for just one thing ... **the Bible!**

The Bible is the revelation of the Creator God, and therefore is not of the world, nor a part of Satan's World System. And that is why it is so hated by the various personal and institutional components of The System. On the human part, there is offended pride and belittled ego. To be told that one is a mere befooled puppet, jerking on the end of an angelic string, is not flattering to a Harvard Ph.D. with an I.Q. of 170, nor reassuring to a Head of State, upon whose brow uneasy lies the crown to start with.

On the angelic part, however, there is far more than ego at stake, though that, too, to be sure. Beyond ego, there is deadly danger. *For, in this one Book is revealed what Satan and his princelings have successfully sequestered from all the rest of the universe accessible to mankind — Satan's Plan and Method for the World System.*

BIBLE NAMES MEAN SOMETHING

Bible names mean something, and are worthy of study. For instance, in *Genesis* 29:32-30;24, the 12 sons of Jacob are named, together with an explanation of their names. Nabal the Fool, for that is the meaning of his name and so he was, is described in *I Samuel* 25:1-25. Numerous other examples could be cited, but the most important are those concerning the name of the Lord Jesus Christ. In *Matthew* 1:21 the name of "Jesus" is said to mean, "he shall save his people *from* their sins." And two verses later, "Immanuel" is interpreted as "God with us."

Bible names are important, and repeatedly reward the student of their meanings with insight as to the history of the people or subjects named. So it is with Satan's Plan and Method for the World System. We know that Satan is the Prince of this world, and that he rules the nations through angelic princes over each nation. A word study of the names involved in the *very first* Satanic kingdom reveals the modus operandi of The Prince of This World.

AFTER THE FLOOD

Many years after the flood of Noah destroyed the old world, his descendants moved en masse into the land of Shinar, the alluvial plain of the Tigris and Euphrates rivers. There, the first kingdom of the new world was founded. We read about it in *Genesis* 10:8-10:

"And Cush begat Nimrod: he began to be a mighty one in the earth. He was a mighty hunter before the Lord: And **the beginning of his kingdom** was Babel, and Erech, and Accad, and Calneh, in the land of Shinar."

This first of Satan's kingdoms in the post-Flood world furnishes a blueprint for world domination; this is "the beginning of his kingdom." As such, it must of necessity also be the beginning of Satan's Plan and Method for the World System. The key is in the meaning of the names of Shinar and the four cities.

The word study below will refer to *Strong's Exhaustive Concordance*, and the *Hebrew Lexicon* it contains. The index numbers of the words in the lexicon are referred as follows: SH 8132 means "*Strong's Hebrew Lexicon*, Reference Number 8132." More complete sources than Strong's Concordance were used in this study, but it provides a convenient and useful means of double-checking and confirmation for most people.

MEANINGS OF THE WORDS

SHINAR, SH 8152. This word is usually thought to be of foreign origin to Hebrew. However, a study of possible Hebrew roots is very informative. Hebrew roots are normally formed with three consonants, the first two remaining in the word, the third occasionally dropped under certain conditions. A careful survey of the Hebrew roots containing the consonants in the word *shinar* (which can be followed visually by using a *Strong's Concordance*) shows two that are highly fitting: *shana* SH 8132, "to alter, change" and *arab* SH 6148, "to mix" (from *Genesius' Hebrew and Chaldee Lexicon*). If *shinar* SH 8152 is of Hebrew origin, its most likely meaning is "to change by mixing and mingling."

BABEL, SH 894. Its meaning is, "confusion;" it is derived from a word meaning "to overflow."

EREK, SH 751. Its meaning is, "length, expanse." It is derived from *arak* SH 748, meaning "to make long, to extend, to stretch out."

ACCAD, SH 390. It means "a fortress," and is derived from an unused root meaning, "to bind; hence, to fortify, strengthen a city" (from *Gesenius' Hebrew and Chaldee Lexicon*).

CALNEH, SH 3641. This word is also usually thought to be of foreign origin to Hebrew. But again, a study of possible Hebrew origins is quite enlightening. The word *Kol*, SH 3605, "the whole, all, every" is almost alone likely as the source of the first syllable (*cal-*). It is derived from *kahal* SH 3634, "to complete." The most likely origin of the second syllable (-neh) is *nahaq*, SH 5090, a root defined as, "Causative — to urge on in a course, to drive (beasts); to lead or drive (a flock), *Genesis* 31:18; to drive away (cattle), *Job* 24:3; to lead away (captives), *I Samuel* 30:2, *Isaiah* 20:4 [from *Gesenius' Hebrew and Chaldee Lexicon*]." Possibly, the origin of the second syllable is *nahal* SH 5095, a root meaning "to lead, specifically, to lead to water." Interestingly, the essential meaning of these two roots is identical. Therefore, if *Calneh* SH 3641 is of Hebrew origin, its most likely meaning is "to drive or herd all [human beings] like cattle."

INTERPRETATION OF THE NAMES

The land and the cities are "the beginning of his kingdom." As such, they constitute a cohesive, integrated, political entity. To accurately apply the Bible pattern of learning from the meaning of names, we must consider the names as an interrelated group or set. We will recognize three elements in Satan's Plan: The Blueprint, The Method, and The Ultimate Goal.

The land of Shinar was the location of the four cities which were "the beginning of his kingdom." It was the background against which the drama was played out. *Shinar* means "to change by mixing and mingling." Since a kingdom is a form of government, and government is an 'order,' we see order being imposed where it was previously absent. Thus, there is 'change' from disorder to order, and it is brought about by 'mixing and mingling.' Regardless of what manner of order, if any, existed previously, if there is mixing and mingling before the new order is imposed, then there is order arising out of chaos.

From chaos comes order. Probably most readers are familiar with this concept under its *scientific* label — Evolution, the official government school doctrine that there is no creator, everything sort of accidentally fell together out of primordial chaos into the orderly world we see around us. Students of political history may recognize this concept by its *philosophical* label, Dialectical Materialism. This doctrine teaches that, out of the conflict between the old order (Thesis) and the forces for *change* (Antithesis) comes the new order (Synthesis), which is neither, but is composed of elements of both (mixing and mingling, you see). **Socialist Radicals, including those rioting in the streets, applauding in the news media, approving in the universities, and cooperating in the government, call this Revolution by Evolution. Politically, the process is simply one of turning a given orderly society into chaos, by a mixing and mingling of contrary ideologies and methodologies, until it breaks down into anarchy. Then, the desperate people will accept any New Order that the power brokers wish to impose.** Satan used this blueprint to impose what historians call Temple

SATAN'S PLAN

Communism upon the free people in Shinar, the result being the beginning of Nimrod's kingdom. Therefore, the meaning of *Shinar* gives us **Satan's Blueprint for World Domination — Dialectical Materialism**, thesis versus antithesis produces synthesis.

SATAN'S METHOD FOR WORLD DOMINATION

The names of the first three cities reveals Satan's Method for World Domination. Babel ("confusion"), Erech ("length, expanse"), and Accad ("a fortress"). Remember, all this takes place "in the land of Shinar," that is, change by mixing and mingling. First, escalating confusion is created, leading to the breakdown of law and order in the target culture (Babel). *Next, when the populace has become desperate enough to permit it, or even demand it, martial law (Accad) is imposed to "restore order," which will turn out to be the New Order.* From this point on, the military will remain very much an enforcing arm of the New Order. Finally, this pattern of confusion to produce anarchy to justify military rule is repeatedly extended (Erech) into one target area after another. In this manner, nations, then regions, then continents, and finally the whole world will be brought under Satan's angelic princelings and subjugated by the New Order. Every major and most minor revolutions in the last two centuries, and every one in this century, has followed this pattern. Therefore, the meaning of the names of the three cities, Babel, Accad, and Erech, gives us **Satan's Method for World Domination** — fomented anarchy, justifying military rule, extended repeatedly.

And where is all this headed? The last city in the "beginning of his kingdom" provides the answer. Remember the derivation of the compound name *Calneh*. *Kol*, meaning "the whole, all, every" plus *nahaq*, a root meaning, "to urge on in a course, to drive (beasts); to lead or drive (a flock); to drive away (cattle); to lead away (captives)."

THE GOAL, HUMAN BESTIALITY

The goal is, first, to reduce all human beings (kol) to bestiality. Drugs, free sex, unrestricted murder of the most innocent of people, little babies, under the euphemism "abortion," lawsuits for every whim, open perversions and depravity — increasing amidst approval by the public. *And why is this so vitally important to Satan's Plan?*

Simple! Depraved, sub-human beasts cannot rule themselves. They must be penned and herded, for their own safety, and for the benefit of their masters (nahaq).

There is a second, more subtle, and far more horrifying purpose for bestializing the human race. Such a depraved populace must suffer a substantial drop in average intelligence over a period of time. *If those intended to be the masters are simultaneously cultured and bred selectively, their average intelligence must as surely increase, and that inexorably.* The result can only be a human race composed of two dominant strains. The one, highly intelligent and competent lords of power. *The other, mere depraved, sub-human beasts, driven like the lower animals by their needs and lusts, and reduced to a state of mental incompetence insufficient to ever successfully challenge their rulers. Such rulers over such subjects need nevermore fear successful revolt — it would be impossible, both technologically and intellectually.*

CLOSING THOUGHTS

I repeat once more: **If** there is a Creator God, and **if** the Bible is His revelation to Mankind, **then** *this is the way things really are.* To assume things are any different, is to run the risk of sticking one's neck into a shackle that is being forged which may never be struck off.

RELIGION IS THE ESSENCE OF HISTORY

Many people wish to pretend that religion has nothing to do with history or reality. *In fact, religion is the essence of history.* All history is a record of the battle between Good and Evil. Good requires morality and hard work; Evil permits and encourages depravity, perversion, and stealing the fruits of other men's labors. Anthropologist J.D. Unwin researched a careful study of the 88 major civilizations that have existed in history. *A similar cycle was observed in each. Every Civilization began upon a foundation of strict morality, and ended with an orgy of moral depravity.* Unwin found that every civilization which embraced immorality and debauchery perished. *There have been no exceptions.*

And there you have it, Satan's plan for world domination. You have but two options: Believe it and oppose it, or disbelieve it and be a part of it. *You will, inevitably and unavoidably, do one or the other.*

Chapter 6

MAN: A NATURAL CONSPIRATOR

Conspiracies are not new. They are, in fact, older than man himself. As we saw in chapter 5, Lucifer, the covering cherub of God, became the first conspirator in recorded history when he — with one third of the angelic host — unsuccessfully attempted to wrest control of the universe from Almighty God. Later, Lucifer became known as Satan or The Adversary.

On a personal and individual level, we are all — to one extent or another — born conspirators. In fact, it would probably be true to say that the 6,000-year history of mankind is largely one of conspiracies — one of plots and counter plots. We shouldn't be surprised; these are merely a manifestation of the jealousy, vanity, lust and greed that is part and parcel of our fallen human nature.

One has only to observe young children to prove the point; they frequently devise plots and schemes designed to put one over on their elders and thus get their own way. Most of their childish ploys may be "cute" and the source of many a good laugh; their schemes are, however, good examples of human nature in action.

When at last we take a good, close, honest look at ourselves we will become increasingly aware that these same proclivities still lurk in the hearts of all of us. The only difference between grownups and children is the fact that the latter are usually somewhat more sophisticated in the practice of their deceptiveness. In their every day affairs they habitually use facts, emphasize facts, bear down on facts, slide off facts, quietly ignore facts and — above all — interpret facts in such a way as to promote their own agenda. They do this with anything but true objectivity in mind. *In other words, human nature truly is a constant!*

As Sir Winston Churchill once observed, "Most people, sometime in their lives, stumble across the truth. Most jump up, brush themselves off, and hurry on about their business as if nothing had happened." People just don't want to face the plain truth about themselves and their inherent wickedness.

"DECEITFUL ABOVE ALL THINGS"

In this regard, two particularly revealing scriptures are found, one in the Old Testament, the second in the New. They both give a stunningly accurate evaluation of the human condition; both are statements of fact — of things the way they really are! In his word, God tells us that "the heart **is** deceitful above all things, and desperately wicked: who can know it?" (*Jeremiah* 17:9). Notice that there is no equivocation in this statement; there are no ifs, maybes, possiblies, or could bes to play around with. It's a plain statement of fact! Notice also the last four words, "who can know it?" The obvious implication is that one cannot even begin to comprehend the depth of mankind's deceitfulness unless and until it is revealed to them by God. That truth is hard for most people to accept.

Now we turn to the New Testament: "[T]he carnal mind **is** enmity against God: for it **is not** subject to the law of God, **neither indeed can be**" (*Romans* 8:7). Again, notice three statements of fact: (1) Our normal, fleshly minds are — by their very nature — opposed to God and his will; (2) Our natural minds are not subject to (i.e., they do not intuitively or spontaneously "owe allegiance to ... or [are] governed by" God's laws (*American Dictionary of the English Language*, Noah Webster, 1828). And, (3) This statement is also vitally important. Here we learn that our natural minds "indeed [in reality and in truth]

MAN: A NATURAL CONSPIRATOR 47

cannot be" subject to God and his will. Again, no equivocation — no if, buts or ands!

The truth is clear — it's simple and straightforward. Unless the Sovereign, Creator God by his grace opens up our minds and our hearts to this basic reality, and then calls us, individually, to repentance — and to be his people — we will remain in our wretched condition. However, in the Lord Jesus Christ (**the** way, **the** truth and **the** life (*John* 14:6), God has provided the way to "save his people from their sins" (*Matthew* 1:21). That is why the Apostle Paul wrote to the saints at Ephesus: "For by grace are ye saved through faith; and that **not** of yourselves: it [salvation] is the gift of God.

"Not of works [things we have done], lest any man should boast" (*Ephesians* 2:8,9).

It should also be noted that, in Biblical terms, repentance is not just being sorry over what we have done. Biblical repentance springs from our seeing and acknowledging ourselves, personally and individually, as we truly are — and then responding to the sovereign call of God through the leading of the Holy Spirit.

In other words, we must not only repent of what we do, but we must, most importantly, repent of what we are.

To fully grasp this reality, we must clearly see and understand that what we **do** is merely a reflection of what we **are**! As scripture states, "For out of the heart [remember *Jeremiah* 17:9?] proceed evil thoughts, murders, adulteries, fornications, thefts, blasphemies;

"These are the things which defile a man ... (*Matthew* 15:19,20)

Thus, we can see that unless God intervenes in our lives we have no real hope of either combatting or successfully overcoming "all that is in the world, the lust of the flesh, and the lust of the eyes, and the pride of life. [All these things are] not of the Father, but [are] of the world" (I *John* 2:16). *Thus, it can truly be said that Christianity is 100 percent supernatural!* Anything else, such as humanistically-inspired "behavior modification," is just another form of artificial respiration. Therefore, all such counterfeit efforts to achieve the "abundant life" (*John* 10:10) in any manner other than that laid out in scripture, are diabolical in nature and thus doomed to failure.

In the final analysis, there is only **one** Way, **one** Truth, and **one** Source of Life: Jesus Christ (*John* 14:6). The Lord Jesus Christ, to whom has been given "all power ... in heaven and earth" (*Matthew* 28:18), is the only "door" through whom one can go in order to come to God. Anyone who teaches "some other way, the same is a thief and a liar" (*John* 10:1,7-12).

Scripture plainly reveals that there are only two types of people: those who are "in Adam" (representing fallen man) and those who are "in Christ." "In Adam all die, even so in Christ [through redemption and salvation] shall all be made alive" (I *Corinthians* 15:22).

SATANIC PITCH

Down through the centuries "that old serpent, the Devil, and Satan, which deceiveth the whole world" (*Revelation* 12:9) has made his pitch to many men who wanted to be considered "great" — individuals who had a tremendous lust to make a name for themselves and exercise great authority over their fellow man. Men such as Nimrod, Pharaoh, Alexander, Nero, Genghis Khan, Napoleon, and — in this century — Roosevelt, Hitler, Stalin, and Mao immediately spring to mind. All attained positions of great power, and then marinated their respective worlds in blood and human misery. Has any good come of their accumulated efforts? Though all made great "names" for themselves, they also ended up on the garbage dump of history as abject failures. However, it can be objectively stated that their lives were not altogether in vain; they can all be used as hideous examples of the way **not** to go!

Of course, Satan also "pitches" all of us from time to time in what he perceives to be our weak points — those areas of our human nature (jealousy, vanity, lust and greed) at which he believes we are most vulnerable. Through glowing promises and enticements, and by means of highly skilled "pitch men" (be they in person, or writers of books and articles, or other means), he can easily induce, seduce, and manipulate most people into frequently falling for his ploys. If any additional proof is needed, just look around you in society — politics, religion, business, and sports — or at your own personal life.

ULTIMATE AUTHORITY
IN MANIPULATION

Satan is the world's ultimate authority on the manipulation and destructive uses of human nature; he can play it like a violin maestro plays his instrument. When we give him a foothold, the old serpent can find and fully exploit weaknesses we never even realized we had.

How then "shall [we] be able to quench all the fiery darts of the evil" one? Consider the example of Jesus.

TEMPTATIONS OF JESUS

Biblical history records that Satan tried out a number of his diabolical "pitches" on Jesus in an attempt to destroy him. We read about this in Matthew's gospel, chapter four.

Matthew records that after Jesus had fasted in the wilderness for forty days and forty nights, the tempter (Satan) came to him with a number of propositions. The first was that if Jesus were truly the Son of God he should turn the stones into food, and thus be able to obtain nourishment following his lengthy abstinence. After all, hadn't God promised to honor such a request?

Notice Jesus' response. Although he knew he **could** have done exactly what Satan tempted him to do, he replied: "It is written, Man shall not live by bread alone, but by every word that proceeds out of the mouth of God" (v.4). Simple. Direct. Powerful. And totally successful. Jesus had his priorities straight. He knew who was calling the shots — and it wasn't Satan!

Again, notice. The devil took Jesus into the holy city and set him on a pinnacle of the temple (v.5). Again he quoted scripture. Watch the spin he puts on God's word; also his use of the word "if": "**If you be the Son of God, cast yourself down:** *for it is written*, He shall give his angels charge concerning you: and in their hands they shall bear you up, lest at any time you dash your foot against a stone" (v.6).

The quotation was correct, but out of context; Satan had given it a twist. Satan tempted Jesus to "prove" himself by showing what a "great" and powerful man he was. Jesus immediately recognized Satan's ploy — Satan's appeal to his manhood, his masculinity, and any ego and vanity he might possess! Jesus was not impressed. In his reply, he put everything perfectly in perspective: "It is written again, You shall not tempt the Lord your God." Although he again recognized that this was, in fact, a promise made by God, he also recognized that if he did what Satan suggested he would be tempting God. God's promise only applied if such an occurrence was accidental.

Pay particular attention to "pitch" number three. The first two had just been warm-ups for the pitch that had struck out practically every other person on earth who had been on the receiving end. This was his master pitch, the one Satan considered — and, in fact, still considers

— by far his best. This was his 110 m.p.h. fast ball that rose startlingly as it approached its mark; he considered it a sure winner.

"Again, the devil took him up into an exceeding high mountain, and showed him all the kingdoms of the world, and the glory of them;

"And said unto him, All these things will I give you, if you will fall down and worship me" (vs.8-9).

Notice something else of vital importance. At no time did Jesus challenge the veracity of Satan's proposition. At no time did Jesus call Satan a liar and claim that "all the kingdoms of the world" were not his to give away as he saw fit. Never once did Jesus dispute the fact that Satan had both the authority and ability to do what he promised. Jesus knew Satan was speaking the truth; he truly had that power.

"IT IS WRITTEN"

Pay particular attention to Jesus' succinct response. It was devastating in its accuracy and directness: "Get away, Satan: *for it is written*, You shall worship the Lord your God, and him only shall you serve" (v.10). Again, his response was condensed, focused — and right on target. Jesus once again let the word of God (which is "quick and powerful, and sharper than any two-edged sword, piercing even to the dividing asunder of soul and spirit, and of the joints and marrow, and is a discerner of the thoughts and intents of the heart" (*Hebrews* 4:12) be his defense.

The truth had a catastrophic effect on Satan's proposition. Like a stake through the heart, it snuffed it out instantly.

Through the power of God, *and by the correct understanding and application of God's word*, Jesus had won a tremendous victory over Satan and the powers of evil.

SATAN CONQUERED

Later — through his life, death, and resurrection — Jesus totally conquered Satan and became Redeemer, Savior, Lord of lords, and King of kings. In the Great Showdown at the end of time, the risen, reigning, Lord Jesus Christ "shall [finally, once and for all time] put down all rule and all authority and power.

"For he must reign till he has put all enemies under his feet" (*I Corinthians* 15:24,25). What happens then will be covered in the final chapter.

ADAM WEISHAUPT

Down through the millennia of human history "that old serpent the Devil, and Satan, which deceives the whole world" (*Revelation* 12:9) has done a masterful job of duping and controlling mankind; his "handiwork" may be seen in abundance at every point of the compass.

But stop and think. The scripture just quoted clearly states that Satan has "deceive[d] the whole world." If the **whole** world is deceived, what part of the world is **not** deceived? It should be abundantly evident that there is no man, woman, child, group, or organization which is not deceived to one degree or another. All means **all**! We are all subject to deception. Only God's Word — in both written and Personal forms — is truth (*John* 14:6;17:17).

As pointed out earlier we are all, by nature, conspirators at heart. From the dawn of time, Satan has sought out — to do his will and implement his plans on earth — those humans who have a particular conspiratorial bent. He frequently works with and through individuals who have a high degree of intelligence and ambition — and who are thus easily manipulatable through their ego, jealousy, vanity, lust, and greed. Adam Weishaupt was one such man.[3]

Adam Weishaupt was an intellectual giant, a brilliant young professor of Canon Law at Ingolstadt University in Bavaria. At age 28, he appeared close to the pinnacle of scholastic accomplishment; it seemed likely that he would, before long, be in charge of one of Europe's great universities and thus live out his life in the glow of spectacular academic achievement. The name Weishaupt would be spoken of with awe in the halls of higher learning.

But this was not to be! Though remarkably young, a grandiose concept had for years been lodged in his brilliantly fertile but devious mind. In his early 20s — as his reputation soared — that marvelous idea kept growing and developing. By his mid 20s, it had blossomed into a brilliantly thought out plan, the impact of which would — in the decades and centuries ahead — shake to its very foundations the old world order. Not only that, the implementation of, and adherence to, his plan would also bring about conditions that would threaten to

---

[3] Sir Walter Scott, in the second volume of *The Life of Napoleon Buonaparte*, tells us that Weishaupt was secretly financed by money barons operating out of Frankfurt, Germany (Rothschild headquarters).

result in the creation of a Weishauptian New World Order by the year 2000 or shortly thereafter.

Contacting the individuals he considered the "creme de la creme" of European intelligentsia, Weishaupt suggested that they get together and work toward the solving of all the problems that had plagued mankind from time immemorial. His "pitch" was diabolical in nature: it was abundantly obvious that only they, with their vastly superior intelligence, understanding, and wisdom had the intellectual genius and long-term vision to give the common rabble what they obviously needed but were too dumb to comprehend.

Of course, having a genius of the caliber of Adam Weishaupt approach them with a challenge of such awesome proportions certainly appealed to their innate sense of superiority; most responded positively. As he gradually revealed more of his magnificent plan, Weishaupt was quickly able to sort out those individuals who could be the most useful in the advancement of his scheme.

Weishaupt was mainly interested in men of like mind — men who thrived on secrecy, intrigue, and manipulation. For leadership positions, he chose only those who had an insatiable lust for power, men who delighted in working behind the scenes while using others as pawns or puppets in the development of their long-term objectives.

MAY DAY, MAY DAY

On May 1, 1776, Weishaupt launched his new elitist organization, the Order of the Illuminati (or the Order of the Enlightened Ones); it was soon to become the most powerful and most secret of the secret societies; those in leadership roles were required to adopt classical names. Weishaupt took the name Spartacus, the leader of an insurrection of slaves in ancient Rome; his chief assistant, Herr von Zwack, counselor to the Prince von Salm, became Cato; Baron Mengenhoffen, Sylla, etc. Since that time May 1, or May Day, has been celebrated by revolutionaries around the world.

It is important that we pay close attention to the name Weishaupt gave to the new organization, The Illuminati. The name is derived from the same root as the word Lucifer, which means bearer of the light, or a being of extraordinary brilliance (*Isaiah* 14:12). It will not escape the attention of the reader that Weishaupt had much the same attitude as Lucifer: "I will ascend ... I will be like the Most High" (vs.14,15).

The *Encyclopedia Britannica*, 11th edition, 1910, tells us that the Order was divided into three main classes. The first two included novices, minervals, and lesser Illuminati; the second consisted of freemasons, ordinary and Scottish Knight; the third or mystery class consisted of two groups, (a) Priest and Regent, and (b) Mages and King. The king was, of course, Weishaupt himself! Any less position would, of course, have been beneath his dignity!

Weishaupt was particularly interested in enrolling young men who were "respectable" and highly thought of. "I cannot use men as they are," he said, "but I must form them." He instructed those who worked closest to him: "Seek the society of young people, watch them, and if one of them pleases you, lay your hands on him." On another occasion, he wrote: "Seek out young and already skilful people.... Our people must be engaging, enterprising, intriguing, and adroit. Above all the first."

On another occasion, Weishaupt wrote Zwack: "My circumstances necessitate that I should remain hidden from most of the members as long as I live. I am obliged to do everything through five or six persons....

"I have two immediately below me into whom I breathe my whole spirit, and each of these two has again two others, and so on. In this way I can set a thousand men in motion and on fire in the simplest manner, and in this way one must impart orders and operate in politics" (*Secret Societies and Subversive Movements*, by Nesta Webster, pp.220,222).

Initiates who made up the outer rings of the Illuminati were told that the great purpose of the Order was "*to make of the human race without any distinction of nation, condition, or profession, one good and happy family.*"

CONGRESS OF WILHELMSBAD

For nearly a decade following its formation, the Illuminati operated behind a thick blanket of secrecy; this was a period of growth and consolidation. Well-known British historian Nesta Webster tells us: "It was in 1777, nearly two years after he had founded the Illuminati, that Weishaupt became a Freemason, and towards the end of 1778 the idea was first launched of amalgamating the two societies....

"But it was not until the Congres de Wilhelmsbad that the alliance between Illuminism and Freemasonry was finally sealed. *This assembly, of which the importance to the subsequent history of the world has never been appreciated by historians*, met for the first time on the 16th of July, 1782, and included representatives of all the secret societies ... which now numbered no less than three million members all over the world. *Amongst these different orders the Illuminati of Bavaria alone had formulated a definite plan of campaign, and it was they who henceforward took the lead.*

"What passed at this terrible Congress will never be known to the outside world, for even those men who had been drawn unwittingly into the movement, and now heard for the first time the real designs of the leaders, were under oath to reveal nothing. One such honest Freemason, the Compte de Virieu ... returning from the Congres de Wilhelmsbad could not conceal his alarm, and when questioned on the 'tragic secrets' he had brought back with him, replied: 'I will not confide them to you. I can only tell you that all this is very much more serious than you think. The conspiracy which is being woven is so well thought out that it will be, so to speak, impossible for the Monarchy and the Church to escape from it.' From this time onwards, says his biographer, M. Costa de Beauregard, '*the Comte de Virieu could only speak of Freemasonry with horror*'" (*World Revolution*, by Nesta Webster, 1921, p.31).

PLOT EXPOSED

First public knowledge of the Illuminati plot to destroy all governments of the world and create a New World Order came to light as the result of an "Act of God." In July 1785, an Illuminati agent named Lanze was galloping on horseback from Frankfurt to Paris. In his possession were documents addressed to the Grand Orient Lodge; these contained important information about the world revolutionary movement, as well as detailed instructions for a planned revolution in France. While traveling near Ratisbon (now Regensberg) the courier was struck by lightning and killed. As a result, the documents fell into the hands of the Bavarian government.

When the Bavarian authorities realized the tremendous significance of their find, they raided the homes of some of the leaders of the Illuminati; thus the Luciferian plot was exposed. Their findings were made public in a book titled, *The Original Writings of the Illuminati*.

Shortly after the founding of the Illuminati, Weishaupt invited John Robison, professor of natural philosophy at Edinburgh University in

Scotland to join his elitist group. This time, Weishaupt completely misjudged his man. Robison, an individual of high moral standards and personal integrity, was not deceived. Although he became closely associated with the "Enlightened Ones," he never became philosophically aligned with them. In 1797, after gathering documentation for a number of years, Robison wrote an explosive expose that laid bare the diabolical plans and inner workings of the Illuminati. His book, *Proofs of a Conspiracy Against all the Religions and Governments of Europe*, was published by William Creech of London.

"PERPETUAL SILENCE AND UNSHAKABLE LOYALTY"

Among other things, Robison revealed that all initiates were required to take a solemn oath "to perpetual silence and unshakable loyalty and submission to the Order, in the person of my superiors; here making a complete surrender of my private judgement, my own will, and every narrow-minded employment of my own power and influence. I pledge myself to account the good of the Order as my own and am ready to serve it with my fortune, my honor and my blood.... The friends and enemies of the Order shall be my friends and enemies; and with respect to both I will conduct myself as directed by the Order ... [and] devote myself to its increase and promotion, and herein to employ all my ability ... without secret reservation" (*Proofs of a Conspiracy*, p.71).

The goals of the Illuminati were both simple and long-term: (1) The abolition of Monarchy and all national governments; (2) The abolition of private property; (3) The abolition of inheritance; (4) The elimination of patriotism; (5) The abolition of all religions; (6) The destruction of the family (i.e., marriage, morality, and the proper education of children), and (7) The creation of a New World Order — a wonderful universal Utopia in which mankind would finally be freed from all the superstitions, prejudices, bigotry, hatreds, fears, and animosities that had plagued it from the dawn of time.

In 1921, Nesta Webster wrote: "With regard to the philanthropic nature of Illuminism, it is only necessary to consult the original writings of Weishaupt to realize the hollowness of the assurance [that Illuminism is merely a philanthropic movement]. Amongst the whole correspondence which passed between Weishaupt and his adepts laid bare by the Government of Bavaria, we find no word of sympathy with the poor or suffering, no hint of social reform, nothing but the desire either for domination, for *world power*, or sheer love of destruction, and throughout all the insatiable spirit of intrigue. *For this purpose every method was held to be justifiable, since the fundamental doctrine of the sect was that 'the end sanctifies the means* (der Zweck heiligt die Mittel),' which Weishaupt referred to in his code, declaring it to be part of the Jesuit system — an imputation which the Abbe Barruel [a French writer who authored *The History of Jacobinism*, another expose of the Illuminati] indignantly denies — and which inevitably led, as Robison pointed out, to the conclusion that "nothing could be scrupled at ... because the great object of the Order was held as superior to every consideration" (*World Revolution*, by Nesta Webster, pp.35,36).

[**Upon reflection, the reader will see that many of the "leaders" in the United States today are basically operating under the same philosophy, that the Order supercedes their national trust**].

CHANGE OF TACTICS

With the massive publicity generated by the exposure of their plot, it became imperative that the name Illuminati be immediately removed from public use. Word was spread that Weishaupt had disbanded his group and that any threat it may have posed to civilization had passed.

That, of course, was a lie. In fact, Professor Robison tells us that Weishaupt wrote to his closest co-conspirators with this advice: "We must consider how we can begin to work under another form. *If only the aim is achieved, it does not matter under what cover it takes place, and a cover is always necessary.* For in concealment lies a great part of our strength. For this reason we must always cover ourselves with the name of another society. The lodges that are under freemasonry are in the meantime the most suitable cloak for our high purpose, for the world is already accustomed to expect nothing great from them that merits attention....

"As in the spiritual Orders of the Roman Church, religion was, alas!, only a pretense, **so must our Order also in a nobler way try to conceal itself behind a learned society or something of the kind.... A society concealed in this manner cannot be worked against. In the case of a persecution or of treason the superiors cannot be discovered.... We shall be shrouded in impenetrable** darkness from spies and emissaries from other societies" (*Secret Societies and Subversive Movements*, by Nesta Webster, 1924, pp.219,220).

In other words, the Illuminati took on the characteristics of a chameleon, changing its colors to whatever hue was necessary to conceal its true identity and further its long-term agenda. Over the last 200 plus years the overall goals of the Illuminati have never changed, although its leaders have used a wide variety of both individuals and groups to further their plans. Many, perhaps most, of the latter have been unwitting pawns in the hands of the master manipulators. Among the diverse groups used early on were "The German Union" and "Amis Reunis" in France.

FRENCH REVOLUTION

In spite of the massive publicity given to the Illuminati plans to foment a bloodbath in France following the discovery of documents on the body of the dead courier, the scheme was never altered.

In 1787 Cardinal Caprari, Apostolic Nuncio in Vienna, wrote a letter to the Pope, pointing out that the activities carried on by the various spin-offs of the Illuminati were increasing: "The danger is approaching, for from all these senseless dreams of Illuminism, of Swedenborgianism, or of Freemasonry a frightful reality will emerge. Visionaries have their time; the revolution they forbode will have its time also."

An even more amazing prediction was made by Marquis de Luchet, a French nobleman who played a part in the revolutionary movement. He recognized the grave danger posed by Illuminism. Early in 1789, he issued this warning:

"Deluded people ... learn that *there exists a conspiracy in favor of despotism against liberty, of incapacity against talent, of vice against virtue, of ignorance against enlightenment.... This society aims at governing the world.* This plan may seem extraordinary, incredible — yes, but not chimerical [merely imaginary] ... no such calamity has ever yet afflicted the world."

Marquis Luchet later warned that if immediate steps were not taken to disarm the threat, the world would see "a series of calamities of which the end is lost in the darkness of time, ... a subterranean fire smoldering eternally and breaking forth periodically in violent and devastating explosions" (*An Essay on the Sect of the Illuminati*, p.vii, quoted in *Secret Societies and Subversive Movements*, by Nesta Webster, 1924, pp.239, 240). What could have more perfectly described the events of the last 200 plus years?

LIGHT BEARERS OF DARKNESS

Within months the blood-drenched French Revolution erupted in all its awesome fury. Tens of thousands were butchered (most guillotined) in an orgy of terror that shook the civilized world to its very foundations. The Illuminati (the Order of the Enlightened Ones, or more correctly, The Light Bearers of Darkness) had taken their first terroristic step toward the fulfillment of their diabolical plan ... the destruction of all national governments and the creation of a New World Order.

The world would never again be the same.

CHAPTER 7

GLOBAL OVERVIEW?

Today, the nations of the world are overloaded with social problems — crime, violence, drugs, debt, and deception. It would appear as if nation after nation is in the process of committing suicide. When World War I, World War II, the Korean and Vietnam wars, and many dozens of other "hot" wars are taken into consideration, it is indisputably true that the twentieth century has proven to be the most violent and bloody century in the history of mankind.

Why? Is all this violence and suffering happening accidentally, or is it the result of a sinister and Machiavellian presence behind the scenes?

As we pursue our quest for knowledge and understanding of what is happening nationally and internationally, we need to recognize, as did the late Dr. Nicholas Murray Butler, President of Columbia University, that "The world is divided into three classes of people: (1) A very small group that **makes** things happen; (2) A somewhat larger group that **watches** things happen, and (3) The great multitude that never knows what happened."

This writer must admit that for many years he was in the last category. When living in England in the mid-1950s, he looked around the world and saw certain events taking place that just didn't make sense to him. He particularly remembers the Suez Crisis and the Hungarian Uprising both of which took place in 1956. He knew that *something* was wrong, but was unable to put his finger on exactly what it was until about fifteen years later.

IMPORTANT LESSON

One of the most important lessons this writer has personally learned over the years is that the decisions one makes in life are only as good as the knowledge upon which they are based. If one starts off with a false premise, one will inevitably end up with an inaccurate conclusion. The information one has may look good, and one may even feel very enthusiastic about it, but unless it is based on truth, on reality — in other words on sound premises — the decisions one makes may prove very costly.

One such example that comes immediately to mind is that of the Mitsubishi Corporation of Japan. In 1988, Mitsubishi was led into purchasing the Rockefeller Center in New York for a vast amount of money. As real estate prices all over the United States were going up, up, and away, it looked like a wonderful investment. Unfortunately for them, Mitsubishi was operating from a number of false premises; among these were the beliefs that the American economy would hold up and that real estate prices would continue to skyrocket.

The *Wall Street Journal* revealed in 1996 that when Mitsubishi finally realized their blunder and sold out in 1994, they lost $2.1 billion on the deal. That's $2,100 million — probably the costliest real estate deal in history.

THE ORDER OF THE ENLIGHTENED ONES

Now, let's take a brief look at world events over the last 200 plus years. Perhaps as we go along you will have some of your own assumptions or premises challenged. All we would ask is that you try to keep an open mind. Then, at the end — when you have heard the evidence — you can make a decision with regard to its veracity. You be the judge.

Two events of tremendous importance took place in 1776. One, of course, was the American Revolution — the event that ultimately led to our freedom from European domination, and the creation of the United States of America.

The second event — one which most people are totally unaware of — took place in Bavaria: the creation of the organization called the Illuminati.

The goals of this — the most secret of the secret societies — was explained in the previous chapter.

As shown in my book *Fourth Reich of the Rich*, very little was outwardly noticeable in the last century by way of fulfilling the various goals of the Illuminati. However, underground or behind the scenes, their agents were busy sowing the seeds that would erupt into a worldwide social revolution.

As Benjamin Disraeli stated in a speech delivered to the British House of Commons on July 15, 1856, "It is useless to deny, because it is impossible to conceal, that a great part of Europe — the whole of Italy and France and a great portion of Germany, to say nothing of other countries — is covered with a network of these secret societies, just as the superficies of the earth are now covered with railroads. And what are their objects? They do not attempt to conceal them. They do not want constitutional government; they do not want ameliorated [improved] institutions. They want to change the tenure of land, to drive out the present owners of the soil and to put an end to ecclesiastical establishments."

The middle of the last century (1848) also saw the publication of Karl Marx's *Communist Manifesto*, the first sentence of which states: "A specter is haunting Europe — the specter of Communism" — one of the outward manifestations of Illuminism.

The various groups developed and grew mostly hidden from public view, and only really began to exert public influence all across Europe at the turn of the twentieth century.

FIVE WORLD IDEOLOGIES

One hundred years ago there were five powerful political ideologies on the world scene vying for space and power. They were:

(1) The secret ideology of international finance centered in "The City" of London. Their aim was and still is to create a One World Government ruled over a closely-knit, well-disciplined group with

special privilege. They and they alone allegedly know what is best for the people of the world.

(2) The Pan-Slavic ideology. Originally conceived by Peter the Great, this basically called for Russian control of eastern Europe ... and the eventual subjugation of all Europe.

(3) The basically Japanese ideology of "Asia for the Asians." This called for a confederation of Asian nations under Japanese control.

(4) The ideology of Pan-Germanism. This called for German control of the European continent, freedom from British restrictions on the high seas, and an open door in the trade and commerce of all the world. And,

(5) Pan-Americanism (or American Isolationism) — the ideology of "America for the Americans." This called for the United States to have political control over the affairs of North, Central, and South America, i.e. control of the Western Hemisphere.

This policy sprang from what is known as the Monroe Doctrine of 1821. The cornerstone of American foreign policy for many years, it was basically a policy of friendship with all other nations, but alliances with none. Any attempt by foreign nations to influence affairs within the American sphere of influence would be viewed as an act of war and dealt with accordingly.

AN INSIDE LOOK AT REALITY

Now, to more clearly understand what has happened — and is now happening — on the international scene, we must first know and recognize the accuracy of statements made by certain well-known leaders on the world stage:

British Prime Minister Benjamin Disraeli in the last century: "[T]he world is governed by very different personages from what is imagined by those who are not behind the scenes."

President Franklin Roosevelt: "In politics, there are no accidents. If it happens you can bet it was planned that way."

Edwin Stanton, Secretary of War in Abraham Lincoln's Cabinet: "Wars are fought, not to defeat an enemy but to create a condition."

ELIMINATING OPPOSITION

The reader will, of course, notice that only ideology #1 (that of "The City" of London and the International Bankers) had the eventual goal of totally destroying the opposition presented by all sovereign nations of the world and forcing them into a One World government — or New World Order.

It is obvious that all of the other ideologies (Pan Slavism, Pan Germanism, Asia for the Asiatics, and American Isolationism) would have to be eliminated if that plan were to be brought to ultimate fruition.

Around the turn of this century, following the unification of numerous German states under Kaiser Wilhelm, Germany became the youngest, most vibrant and ambitious nation in Europe. It was recognized by the international bankers and political leaders that Germany posed a major threat to their plans. In fact, it was recognized by experts that Germany would probably defeat Britain if it came to a war between the two powers. As a result, unprecedented steps had to be taken by Britain to both protect and forward their plans.

BALANCE OF POWER

It should be noted that for many years prior to the beginning of the twentieth century Britain had developed and maintained what was called the "Balance of Power" on the European continent. As outlined by author E. C. Knuth, its purposes were as follows:

(1) Divide the nations of Europe into two antagonistic camps of nearly equal military strength, so as to retain for Britain itself the power to sway a decision either way;

2) To make the leading and potentially most dangerous military power the particular prey of British suppression and to have the second strongest power on the other side. To subsidize the "most Favored Nations" with financial investments, and to permit them to acquire political advantage under the beneficent protection of the British Sea Power, to the disadvantage and at the expense of the nations being suppressed;

(3) To subject the continent of Europe to the policy of encirclement so as to keep the nations of the continent in poverty and ineffectiveness, and thereby prevent the growth of sufficient commercial expansion and wealth to create a rival sea power;

(4) To retain the complete control and hegemony over the seas of the world, which was acquired by defeating the allied fleets of its only real rivals, France and Spain, at Trafalgar in 1805;

(5) To shift this Balance of Power as required so as to be able to strike down friend or foe in the rapidly changing world of power politics, in that inexorable ideology that demands that everything and anything must be sacrificed for the future welfare and expansion to the eventual goal of the empire ... the eventual control of **all** the lands, and **all** the peoples of **all** the world.

In the words of Cecil Rhodes, "**In the end Great Britain is to establish a power so overwhelming that wars must cease and the Millennium be realized**" (*Empire Of "The City,"* by E. C. Knuth, pp. 61, 62).

NICCOLO MACHIEVELLI

As the same author, E. C. Knuth, points out, "The power of International Finance rests upon the doctrine of government advanced by Niccolo Machievelli, which holds that any means, however unscrupulous, may be justifiably employed in order to maintain a strong central government; and this doctrine has always been used as a vindication and mandate of imperialists and dictators, and it cannot gain a foothold unless the forces of freedom have become undermined and are no longer able to offer open opposition....

"The findings of Machiavelli and other students of power decree that to obtain power it is essential to ignore the moral laws of man and of God; that promises must be made only with the intention to deceive and mislead others to sacrifice their own interests; that the most brutal atrocity must be committed as a matter of mere convenience; that friends or allies must be betrayed as a matter of course as soon as they have served their purpose. But it is also decreed that these atrocities be kept hidden from the common people except only where they are of use to strike terror to the hearts of opponents; that there must be kept up a spurious aspect of benevolence and benefit for the greater number of the people, and even an aspect of humility to gain as much help as possible" (*The Empire of "the City,"* by E.K.Knuth, pp.96, 76).

PLAYING OFF NATIONS

To keep control, Britain frequently played off one European nation against another. If one nation appeared to be getting strong enough to pose a possible threat to its control of Europe, Britain would create problems for that nation and organize other nations against it. Britain would then arrange financing for those nations and then ensure that financing was withheld from the nation that Britain wanted to limit and control.

For many years whichever side was backed by Britain proved to be the eventual winner. In this manner, through their Balance of Power, the Britain controlled Europe.

THE EMERGENCE OF GERMANY

The emergence of Germany as an industrial, economic and military power in the 1890s and early 1900s posed a unique threat to Britain and the international bankers. It became obvious that something extraordinary had to be done to prevent Germany from destroying the Balance of Power and becoming the dominant force in Europe.

Writing in *The Round Table* in August 1911, Philip Kerr (Lord Lothian) declared, "There are at present two codes of international morality — the British or Anglo-Saxon and the continental or German. Both cannot prevail. If the British empire is not strong enough to be a real influence for fair dealing between nations, the reactionary standards of the German bureaucracy will triumph, and it will then only be a matter of time before the British Empire itself is victimized by an international 'holdup'.... *Unless the British people are strong enough to make it impossible for backward rivals to attack them with any prospect of success, they will have to accept the political standards of the aggressive military powers.*"

THE PILGRIM SOCIETY

What happened next on the international scene is of tremendous significance. If we are to understand world affairs over the last 100 years, we must understand the truth about a vitally important secret treaty: we refer to the founding in London on July 24, 1902 of The Pilgrim Society. A similar society was established in New York on January 13, 1903.

The Pilgrim Society was made up of the elite from the Establishment (the leaders in society, finance, industry, and politics) in both Britain and the United States. Their basic, long-term goals were expressed by Andrew Carnegie, the American multimillionaire, and by Cecil Rhodes of Britain who made a vast fortune in South African gold, that is, unite Britain and America with the ultimate goal of creating a World Government under British control.

Their most important, short-term purpose, however, was the protection of Britain, or more particularly the virtually unseen empire of what is called "The City" of London, England. This is the nerve center from which is controlled most of the financial, political, and military affairs of the world. To use a chess analogy, the nations of the world have been and are being used by "The City" like pawns in the game of chess.

Financial power, political power, and financial and political control of the world scene are their all-consuming goals.

It is almost impossible to find reference to the Pilgrim Society in American literature; yet it is undoubtedly among the most powerful secret societies in the world. Fleeting reference is made to it in a few obscure books. In the United States it is overtly known as the Anglo-American Establishment; its members are the primary "movers and shakers" of American society — the ones in whose hands presently rest control of finance, business, politics, education and the media.

The American Heritage Dictionary defines the Establishment as "an exclusive group of powerful people who run a government or society by means of private agreements or decisions."

DR. CARROLL QUIGLEY

The late Professor Carroll Quigley, of Georgetown University in Washington, D.C. wrote a book about some of the activities of this elitist group; it is titled, *The Anglo-American Establishment*. Incidentally, Professor Quigley was the mentor of a young man named Bill Clinton when he was a student at Georgetown during the 1960s.

In another book, *Tragedy and Hope*, published in 1966, Professor Quigley also referred to this group as "an international Anglophile network." On the same page, page 950, he wrote: "I know of the operations of this network because I studied it for twenty years and was permitted for two years, in the early 1960s, to examine its papers and secret records. I have no aversion to it or to most of its aims.... *[M]y chief difference of opinion is that it wishes to remain unknown."*

The "Eastern Establishment [is] really above parties and [is] much more interested in policies than with party victories. They [have] been the dominant element in both parties since 1900.... They [are] Anglophile, cosmopolitan, Ivy League, internationalist, astonishingly liberal, patrons of the arts, and relatively humanitarian. All these things [make] them anathema to the lower-middle-class and petty-bourgeois class, chiefly in small towns and in the Middle West...." (pp.1244-5).

Quigley supplies further background information on this international Anglophile network. On page 132, we read: "In 1919 they founded the Royal Institute of International Affairs (Chatham House) for which the chief financial supporters were Sir Abe Bailey and the Astor family (owners of *The Times of London*). *Similar Institutes of Foreign Affairs were established in the chief British dominions and in the United States (where it is known as the Council on Foreign Relations)* in the period 1919-1927." In a book by the same name, former FBI agent Dan Smoot described the Council on Foreign Relations (CFR) as America's "Invisible Government."

In 1922, Mayor John H. Hylan of New York, declared: "The real threat to our Republic is the invisible government which, like a giant octopus, sprawls its slimy length over our city, state and nation. At the head is a small group of banking houses generally referred to as 'international bankers.' This little coterie of powerful international bankers run our government for their own selfish ends."

Former CFR member Rear Admiral Chester Ward tells us that, "*Once the ruling members of the CFR have decided that the U.S. Government should adopt a particular policy, the very substantial resource facilities of the CFR are put to work to develop arguments, intellectual and emotional, to support the new policy, and to confound and discredit, intellectually and politically, any opposition.*

"Previous attempts to document the CFR's influence have been ignored or smeared by the liberal press as exaggerated. This is to be expected, considering the beachheads that key CFR members hold in all parts of the media, and especially because any attempt to tell about the power of the CFR is bound to sound exaggerated. *Actually, all the published reports thus far have underestimated the CFR's influence*, just as all previous accounts of Henry Kissinger's power vastly underestimate him" (*Kissinger on the Couch*, by Rear Admiral Chester Ward, with Phyllis Schlafly, p.148). The Rear Admiral then confirms that, "*The goal of the CFR is submergence of U.S. sovereignty and national independence into an all-powerful one world government ... this lust to surrender the sovereignty and independence of the United States is pervasive throughout most of the membership.*"

"IN A FEUDALISTIC FASHION"

This statement is further substantiated by Professor Quigley who declares that "another far-reaching aim, [is] nothing less than to create a world system of financial control in private hands able to dominate the political system of each country and the economy of the world as a whole. This system was to be *controlled in a feudalistic fashion* by the central banks of the world [**international bankers**] acting in concert, by secret agreements arrived at in frequent private meetings and conferences" (*Tragedy and Hope*, p.324).

Edith Kermit Roosevelt, columnist and granddaughter of FDR, made the following insightful observation: "Today the path to total dictatorship can be laid by strictly legal means, unseen and unheard by the Congress, the President, or the people.... Outwardly, we have a Constitutional government. We have operating within our government and political system, another body representing *another form of government*, a bureaucratic elite which believes our Constitution is outmoded and is sure that it is on the winning side.

"All the strange developments in foreign policy agreements may be traced to this group who are going to make us over to suit their pleasure.... This political action group has its own political organizations, its own pressure groups, its own vested interests, its foothold within our government, and its own propaganda apparatus."

Those who wish to learn more about how the internationalists took over the United States and are presently running it, should read Dr. Eugene Schroder's book, *Constitution: Fact or Fiction.*

CHAPTER 8

TOP SECRET AGREEMENT

With that background, we return to the early part of the twentieth century. From the outset the "partners" in the Pilgrim Society made a secret agreement among themselves: if Britain ever found itself in danger of losing control of Europe, the United States would come to its rescue.

This top secret agreement was, of course, kept from the American people. Had it been known it would clearly have been recognized as an act of treason on the part of those who made the secret pact.

At that time the vast majority of Americans viewed Britain as an enemy. After all, had not America thrown off the British yoke of bondage a little more than 100 years earlier? The people had no desire to renew those ties. The Monroe Doctrine of independence and isolationism was a declaration of the will of most Americans; any political move that went contrary to that policy would be classified as treason.

The United States Constitution, the Supreme Law of the Land, declared: "**Treason** against the United States shall consist only in levying war against them, or in adhering to her enemies, giving them aid and comfort" (*United States Constitution*, Article 3, Section 3). That would, of course, cover any move by any person or group of persons to undermine American sovereignty and independence.

WORLD WAR I

In the years following the turn of this century German economic and military strength grew steadily. It became clear that Germany would soon overtake Britain and become the new dominant power in Europe.

In 1914, the assassination of Austrian Archduke Franz Ferdinand was used as the pretext to start what is known as World War I. What began on June 28 as a local dispute between Serbia and Austria was manipulated, inside 5 weeks, into a full-scale European war in which Austria, now united with Germany, was pitted against the rest of Europe.

The old Balance of Power ploys were implemented.

World War I, which saw the introduction for the first time in warfare of machine guns and tanks, changed for ever the way in which wars are fought. Losses on both sides were astronomical. In a number of battles hundreds of thousands of troops lost their live in just a few days. This led to trench warfare and a long drawn out struggle.

As 1915 and 1916 came and went conditions grew much worse. The arrival of 1917 found Britain and her allies on the verge of economic ruin. The success of German submarine warfare brought Britain to the point of starvation and imminent military collapse.

After many unsuccessful attempts to drag the United States into this European war, efforts were finally successful in 1917.

TWO VITAL CONNECTIONS

It is vital that we understand the significance of another event that led up to America's entry into the war: That event was the creation of the Federal Reserve private monopoly banking system in 1913. This gave the international bankers control over the American economy; it also served to consolidate the hidden ties between the two powers that existed through the Pilgrim Society.

On January 3, 1917, America broke off diplomatic relations with Germany, and two months later, declared war on that country. This declaration was made despite the fact that 90 percent of the American people were against such a move.

As Sir Harry Brittain wrote in his book, *Pilgrim Partners*, "*At length in April, 1917, dawned a wonderful day in Anglo-American history, the U.S. had joined the Allies....* A few days later a solemn service was held in St. Paul's Cathedral to mark the entry of the United States into the war, and **the members of the Pilgrim Club were allotted a place of honor under the dome, near the king and queen**" (p.115).

The first American troops arrived in Europe on June 26, 1917; within a year more than one million were on European soil. Within months of America's entrance into World War I, Germany's submarine control of the Atlantic had been eliminated and the tide of battle reversed. The war finally ended on November 11 with the collapse of Germany.

DEFEAT OF CZARIST RUSSIA

The defeat of Imperial Germany was just one of the results of WWI. Much more important was the defeat of Czarist Russia, an implacable foe of the bankers.

Apart from the United States, Czarist Russia was the only nation to reject overtures by the international bankers. When the international bankers under the Rothschilds attempted to divide the United States into two during the American Civil War in the 1860s, the Russian Czar sent two fleets — one to New York, the other to San Francisco — to assist Abraham Lincoln to contain the threat to the Monroe Doctrine from Europe. This earned the Czar the unreserved hatred of the money monopolists.

LONG TERM STRATEGIES

Let's backtrack for a few minutes. The international bankers who, for more than 220 years have been financing the move to create a New World Order, have always had long-term strategies.

In the 1800s the British crown expanded its operations in the Orient and, through the infamous Opium War of 1839-42, managed to get a stranglehold on China. As time went by the international bankers realized that they needed a "policeman" in the Orient — a nation which give them the Balance of Power in that area. They chose Japan for that job.

At the end of the last century Britain, Japan, and the United States signed a secret treaty. In 1894, Japan attacked China, and the international bankers — through the House of Sassoon, the Soongs and the House of Mitsiu — took over the Japanese banking system through the Bank of China and Japan.

Shortly thereafter, the British brought in the famous munitions firm of Vickers to build up Japan's armed forces. In 1900 American troops were used in the Boxer rebellion to put down a Chinese uprising against foreign control of the Orient.

EVICTING THE RUSSIANS

The next aim of international finance was the eviction of Russia from the Orient. On February 8, 1904, a Japanese flotilla sailed into Port Arthur and attacked the Russian fleet, inflicting tremendous damage.

Shortly thereafter, under the brilliant leadership of Field Marshal Oyama, the Japanese — though greatly outnumbered — inflicted terrible defeats on the Russians, thus effectively ending Russian influence in that area.

As has historically been the case in dealings with the British, Japan was not well rewarded for her help in eliminating Russian influence. In what undoubtedly included help in removing German influence in the coming and planned World War I, Japan was awarded the German Marianas, Caroline and Marshal groups of islands, stretching about 5,000 miles east and west and 300 miles south and east.

As always, Britain kept the best of the "goodies." In the Orient, control of such strategic ports as Hong Kong, Shanghai, and Canton gave them virtual control of all world trade with China. They took their cut coming and going!

The collapse of Czarist Russia in 1917 — and the subsequent takeover of that nation by the international banker-created and financed Communist regime — successfully removed the threat of Pan-Slavism from the world's political equation. One down and three to go, if the lustful dreams of "The City" were to be fulfilled.

As Dr. Carroll Quigley stated in his book, *Tragedy and Hope*, more changes can be made in the social order during five years of war than during fifty years of peace.

Obviously, other wars were called for.

COOLIDGE BALKS

As documented in *Descent into Slavery?* by this author, agents of the Crown and the international bankers were instrumental in raising up the individuals and in creating the conditions that led to the outbreak of World War II.

In 1928, when President Coolidge refused to allow American ships and troops to be used to put down another wave of nationalism in China, Japan renounced the treaty signed more than 30 years earlier. In 1932, Japan invaded Manchuria and then moved into China, capturing most the major cities and strategic areas.

This obviously shattered British control of the Orient. It also created a situation in which Japan's goal of Asia for the Asiatics, with Japan in control, became a virtual reality.

If the Crown and international bankers were to move forward in their plans to create a New World Order, Japan obviously had to be crushed.

Toward the end of the 1930s, the internationalists — with backing of the Roosevelt administration — tightened the screws on Japan; she was denied access to raw materials and other vital supplies. Japan was gradually being strangled economically.

PEARL HARBOR

Although it was recognized by their military leaders that it meant ultimate defeat, Japan — in order to save face and avoid being humiliated — decided to strike back; their attack on Pearl Harbor on December 7, 1941 was the result.

Incidentally, American intelligence, having broken both Japan's military and diplomatic codes, knew of the impending attack. Despite this fact, most of the American fleet was lined up, like ducks in a shooting gallery, in Pearl Harbor as a further inducement to the Japanese.

When WW II ended in 1945, two of the three remaining obstacles to a New World Order (Germany and Japan) had been removed. Three down. One to go.

ONLY THE UNITED STATES REMAINED

Only the United States of America remained unconquered. It had to be destroyed if the aims of the "The City" and international bankers were to be fulfilled.

Over the last fifty plus years the United States has been under relentless attack by the forces of internationalism. The attacks have come from every point of the compass; we see the effects all around us in society.
How were many of these effects accomplished?

REPORT FROM IRON MOUNTAIN

That question brings us to a small, but very important book: *Report From Iron Mountain*. It was published by The Dial Press, New York, in 1966.

Some background: In the early 1960s, people at the highest levels of political and economic power in Washington and New York sought methods by which their long-term political agenda might be speeded up. As a result, early in August, 1963, an agent approached 15 already proven experts in various fields to say they had been selected to serve on a commission "of the highest importance." They were all American citizens.

The first meeting of the Special Study Group was held at a place called Iron Mountain in New York State in August, 1963. To throw off any snoops, the various experts used false names. Later, they met on the average once a month; usually at weekends, and usually for two days. The group met all over the country, always at a different place, except for the first and last times, which were at Iron Mountain. They never met in Washington, or on government property. Although the participants took notes for their own use, there were no minutes of the meetings.

At the initial meeting at Iron Mountain, these specialists were given an important assignment: Their goal, ostensibly, was to devise methods whereby conditions could be created that would result in "permanent peace." When stripped of all *newspeak*, however, the declared desire for "permanent peace" was, in fact, a euphemism for the ultimate elimination of all opposition to their true agenda — the creation of a New World Order.

MANIPULATIVE GUISE

Traditionally, governments have used wars to defeat their enemies and to manipulate and control their own people under the guise of "patriotism." A "different kind of thinking" was needed. Different kinds of wars (or what William James described as "the moral equivalent of war") were needed that would accomplish the same objectives: bigger government, bigger debt, and more control over the population. There was to be "no agonizing over cultural or religious values. No moral posturing" (foreword, p.xx).

[The existence of the *Report* was first disclosed when one of the group, a man known only as "John Doe," chose to reveal it to a friend and author, Leonard C. Lewin in 1966. The *Report* was given to Lewin "with the express understanding that if for any reason I was unwilling to become involved, I would say nothing about it to anyone else" (foreword, p.x). The book was published a year later].

"ALTERNATE ENEMIES"

In its final *Report*, presented in 1966, the Group stated that: "An acceptable surrogate for the war system [would] require the *expenditure of resources for completely nonproductive purposes* at a level comparable to that of the military expenditures otherwise demanded by the size and complexity of each society. Such a substitute system of apparent `waste' *must* be of a nature that will permit it to remain independent of the normal supply-demand economy; *it must be subject to arbitrary political control....*

"[A] *credible* substitute for war must generate *an omnipresent and readily understood fear of personal destruction.* This fear must be of a nature and degree sufficient to *ensure adherence* to societal values to the full extent that they are acknowledged *to transcend the value of individual human life*" (p.83).

" *The war system makes the stable government of societies possible.* It does this by essentially providing an *external necessity for a society to accept political rule.* In so doing, it establishes the basis for ... *the authority of government to control its constituents....*

"[A]n effective political substitute for war would require `*alternate enemies,*' some of which might seem equally farfetched in the context of the current war system" (p.64,66).

"*Credibility, in fact, lies at the heart of the problem of developing a political substitute for war....*" (p.66).

NO MERE SYMBOLIC CHARADE

Elsewhere, the *Report* states that "a viable substitute for war as a social system cannot be a mere symbolic charade. It must involve real risk of real personal destruction, and on a scale consistent with the size and complexity of modern social systems. *Credibility is the key.* Whether the substitute is ritual in nature or functionally substantive, *unless it provides a believable life-and-death threat* it will *not* serve the socially organizing function of war.

"The existence of an *accepted* external menace, then, is essential to social cohesiveness as well as to the acceptance of political authority. *The menace must be believable*, it must be of a magnitude consistent with the complexity of the society threatened, and *it must appear, at least, to affect the whole society*" (p.47).

But who would be capable of beginning the con of the American people in this manner?

LYNDON BAYNES JOHNSON

On the American political scene at that time, there was no one more highly qualified to begin to implement the recommendations of this diabolical *Report* than the nefarious Texan, Lyndon Baynes Johnson. As a liberal political trickster and legislative con artist par excellence, LBJ had few peers. As a salesman, he was superb.

Johnson first went to Washington in 1937 when he won a contest to fill a vacancy caused by the death of a representative. In 1938 he was elected to a full term, after which he was returned for 4 terms. He was elected U.S. senator in 1948, and reelected in 1952. He became Democratic leader in 1953.

In 1961, when John. F. Kennedy became president, LBJ, his running mate, became vice-president. Upon Kennedy's assassination on November 22, 1963, Johnson became president.

Shortly thereafter, in an interview with Robert Spivak, he stated: "You say I am not a liberal. Let me tell you I am more liberal than Eleanor Roosevelt, and I will prove it to you. Franklin D. Roosevelt was my hero — he gave me my start" (*New York Herald Tribune*, 12/1/63). With his socialistic Great Society agenda — and his initial implementation of the recommendations set forward in the *Report From Iron Mountain* — he certainly did "prove" that fact during his five plus years in the Oval Office.

RECOMMENDATIONS IMPLEMENTED

When, in the light of the *Report from Iron Mountain*, we examine various policies implemented by the federal government over the last

35 years, we see very clearly that the recommendations have been, and still are being implemented.

Since 1963 we have seen the federal government engaged in a long series of "wars," all of which are accomplishing the goals outlined in the *Report.* America has seen "wars" declared on poverty, drugs, crime, and inflation. We have seen myriad wars declared on an alleged energy crisis, and on the alleged destroyers of our environment.

Regarding the latter, the *Report* states: "It may be ... that gross pollution of the environment can eventually replace the possibility of mass destruction by nuclear weapons **as the principal apparent threat** to the survival of the species.... [I]t constitutes a threat that can be dealt with only through **social organization and political power.**

"It is true that the rate of pollution could be increased selectively for this purpose..... But ... it seems highly improbable that a program of deliberate environmental poisoning could be implemented in a politically acceptable manner....

"It is more probable, in our judgment, that **such a threat will have to be invented**, rather than developed from unknown conditions" (pp.66,67).

Over the years we have also seen war declared on other alleged threats to the American people. These have all been accompanied by massive media campaigns condemning these "enemies" and supporting the New World Order views — and extolling the alleged virtues of such immense expenditures of both manpower and financial resources. As a result of all these "menaces ... being made to appear at least to affect the whole society," the public has been swept along on a tidal wave of ignorant approval.

THE RESULT OF THESE WARS?

Now, stop and think! Have any of these "wars" proven successful? Have they accomplished their alleged goals?

Have we less poverty, or more poverty?
Have we less drug usage, or more drug usage?
Have we less crime, or more crime?
Have we less inflation, or more inflation?
Have we less federal debt, or more federal debt?
Have we less government intrusion, or more government intrusion?
Have we less government control, or more government control?

The record is clear. Since these various "wars" were initiated, we have had a tremendous increase in poverty, drug usage, and crime. We have also seen a huge loss of personal liberties — and a great increase in the size and intrusiveness of civil government. From the point of view of the American people, these and other similar programs have proven catastrophic.

However, when we view them in the light of the *Report from Iron Mountain*, we see that they have, in fact, proven to be resounding successes. You see, as Edwin Stanton, Lincoln's Secretary of War, once observed, "Wars are not fought to defeat an enemy. Wars are fought to create a condition" — one conducive to the further development of their plans. As President Franklin Roosevelt once stated: "In politics, there are no accidents. If it happens, you can bet it was planned that way."

SYSTEMATICALLY DESTROYING THE UNITED STATES

As planned in the early 1960s, these various "wars" are being used to systematically destroy the United States. They have succeeded in greatly enlarging our national debt (now standing at close to $6 Trillion). They have also succeeded in putting unprecedented amounts of power into the hands of Big Brother government.

The bottom line? People Control is the name of the game.

You see, it was planned that way.

CHAPTER 9

WHITE SUPREMACISTS EXPOSED

In recent years the national media has carried many stories harshly condemning as nasty, wicked, and evil any person or organization which, *in their opinion*, is "white supremacist" or "racist."

These smear labels were used to great effect in recent years by *The New York Times*, *The Wall Street Journal*, *U.S.A. Today*, *Time*, *People* magazine and even the federal government, to adversely influence the minds of multiple millions nationwide against such people as Randy Weaver and Kevin Harris (See *Midnight Messenger*, Issues #45,46,50,52). The charges were repeated with such monotonous regularity that they became the prevailing theme of most articles about Weaver and Harris. Thankfully, the jury saw through the lying deceit and acquitted the two men. Both are now free.

Interestingly enough, the terms "white supremacist" and "racist" have loose meanings; they are never defined. However, it is always made perfectly clear that whatever these terms mean (and regardless of the facts), such behavior is nauseatingly repugnant and not to be tolerated in our modern, humanistic, politically correct society.

MANIPULATING MINDS

It should be abundantly evident to any objective observer with access to the facts that the mass media is deliberately manipulating the minds of the general public so that they will be incapable of forming any honest and rational opinions of their own. Even now, most people are fearful of expressing opinions other than those that are politically acceptable at the moment.

This is being done, not as a result of an honest, heartfelt concern for minorities, but rather for purely political reasons. The media and the politicians create opposing forces of opinion. What unfolds is a clear demonstration of the Hegelian Principle in action: Thesis, Antithesis and Synthesis — pressure from one political force and pressure from an opposing sociological force in order to achieve a political objective, a synthesis. As Franklin Roosevelt stated so succinctly, "you can bet it was planned that way."

WILL THE REAL WHITE SUPREMACISTS AND RACISTS PLEASE STAND UP

As has been clearly documented in numerous books in recent years, the movers and shakers of the Eastern Establishment certainly don't underestimate their own value; *as true Illuminists, they unquestionably consider themselves vastly superior to all other groups on earth.* This whole attitude of natural superiority, for example, comes through loud and clear in the writings of the late Dr. Carroll Quigley, one of Bill Clinton's early mentors. As descendants of the Nordic, Anglo-Saxon race, they consider themselves to be God's gift to mankind (one could say, "God's Chosen People"), and thus destined to rule the whole planet in the New World Order (See *Tragedy and Hope* and *The Anglo-American Establishment*).

Although it is generally well hidden, these very powerful individuals and organizations — the true movers and shakers of modern American society — are much more ardent White Supremacists and Racists than the numerically weak and politically impotent individuals whom the Establishment arrogantly tars with the same brush.

Not only so, but they believe — as we shall see from their own documents — that they now have the political and military muscle needed to force their wicked will upon those whom they contemptuously refer to as "Lilliputians of lesser race" or "minor races" — and thus bring into being their long-planned New World Order. The mind manipulating, myth-mongers in the mass media have, it must be admitted, done a marvelous job of deceiving the American public, which now believes the exact opposite of what is actually true. Their incessant and politically-correct charges of white supremacism and racism against others has been very clearly (and very cleverly!) designed to cover up the fact as to who are the real culprits.

As proof of the above statements, we present two documents; these demonstrate the Establishment's elitist, white supremacist, and racist plans in no uncertain terms:

Document #1 is an article, *God's Plan for America*, reproduced in its entirety from the September 1950 issue of *The New Age magazine* (pp. 551-552, Vol. LVIII, No.9), then the official organ of the Supreme Council 33 degree Scottish Rite Freemasonry, Southern Jurisdiction, USA. The title of the magazine has since been changed.

The reader will note from this article that the god of Masonry (euphemistically called Providence) is "dedicated to the unification of all races, religions and creeds. *This plan, dedicated to the new order of things, is to make all things new — a new nation, a new race, a new civilization and a new religion, a nonsectarian religion that has already been recognized and called the religion of 'The Great Light....'*"

[Who is this 'Great Light'? In his book *Morals and Dogma*, Albert Pike, Supreme Grand Commander of the Ancient and Accepted Scottish Rite of Freemasonry, Southern Jurisdiction, at the end of the last century, gives us the plain answer: "Lucifer, [is] the Light-Bearer!.... Lucifer, the Son of the Morning! Is it *he* who bears the *Light*, and with its splendors intolerable blinds feeble, sensual, or selfish souls? Doubt it not!...." (p. 321)].

Continuing the *New Age* magazine article from 1950: "[T]he Nordics are God's chosen people.... Providence has chosen the Nordic [Anglo-Saxon] race to unfold the 'New Age' of the world — a 'Novus Ordo Seclorum'" [New World Order].

"*The Nordics are the highest branch of the fifth Aryan Civilization* ... and the American race will be the sixth *Aryan Civilization.* This

VOL. LVIII, NO. 9

SEPTEMBER, 1950

PRICE 15 CENTS

THE NEW AGE

(Reg. U. S. Pat. Off.)

MAGAZINE

The Official Organ of
The Supreme Council 33° A. & A. Scottish Rite of Freemasonry S. J. U. S. A.
PUBLISHED AT 1735 SIXTEENTH STREET N. W., WASHINGTON, D. C.

WHITE SUPREMACISTS EXPOSED

GOD'S PLAN IN AMERICA

C. WILLIAM SMITH, *New Orleans, La.*

THERE are three plans in action in America today and they all have different purposes. The first plan is God's plan, a nonsectarian plan; the second is the Roman Catholic plan, and this is a denominational or sectarian plan, and the third is the Communistic plan, an anticapitalist plan.

God's plan is dedicated to the unification of all races, religions and creeds. This plan, dedicated to the new order of things, is to make all things new—a new nation, a new race, a new civilization and a new religion, a nonsectarian religion that has already been recognized and called the religion of "The Great Light."

Looking back into history, we can easily see that the Guiding Hand of Providence has chosen the Nordic people to bring in and unfold the new order of the world. Records clearly show that 95 per cent of the colonists were Nordics—Anglo-Saxons.

Providence has chosen the Nordics because the Nordics have prepared themselves and have chosen God. They are not church worshippers, for they worship God's word—the Holy Bible. The Nordics are the great Bible-reading people of the world today, and the Nordics—Anglo-Saxons —were the first people to print the Holy Bible in great quantity, and they were known as the people of a book, that book being the Holy Bible.

But, in order to read the Bible, it is necessary to know how to read. In the Nordic race there is no illiteracy. In Norway there has been no illiteracy for more than a hundred years. Another fact that shows clearly that the Nordics are God's chosen people this time is they are always looking for more light on the mission of life. Looking at their station of life, these great Bible-reading people should open the eyes of the world. King Gustaf of Sweden is a great light in the nonsectarian Masonic Brotherhood, and King Haakon of Norway is a Masonic light in Norway. The late King Christian of Denmark was a Masonic spirit in his Denmark; also King George of England is a Masonic light to his Anglo-Saxon people.

Just as Providence has chosen the Jewish race—the Children of Israel— to bring into the world righteousness by carrying the "Ten Commandments" which emphasize "Remember the Sabbath Day and keep it holy," so also Providence has chosen the Nordic race to unfold the "New Age" of the world—a *"Novus Ordo Seclorum."*

One of the first of the Nordics to reach the New World was the Viking, Leif Ericsson. He sailed from Norway to bring to his people in Iceland a new message, the message of the Christian God. But Providence moves in a mysterious way His wonders to perform, and so Leif the Lucky was sent by Providence to the New World. From the abundance of grapes found there Leif Ericsson called the place Vinland.

It is easy to sense that Leif Ericsson was sent by the Guiding Hand of Providence to bring the Norse spirit of the "All-Father" to the shores of the New World.

The Nordics are the highest branch of the fifth Aryan Civilization. The Latins are of the fourth Aryan Civilization, and the American race will be the sixth Aryan Civilization. This new and great civilization is like an American Beauty rosebud, ready to open and send its wonderful fragrance to all the world.

George Washington, Thomas Jefferson, Benjamin Franklin, John Adams, Thomas Paine and many others of the founders of the new nation in the New World were Nordics.

Thomas Paine, the spark plug of the American Revolution, loved God but hated sectarianism. In "These Are the Times," he wrote: "We have it in our power to begin the world all over again! A situation similar to the present hath

551

THE NEW AGE

not happened since the days of Noah, till now. The birthday of a New World is at hand."

As stated before, God's Plan in America is a nonsectarian plan. Our Constitution is nonsectarian. Our great American Public Schools—God's chosen schools—are nonsectarian. The Great Spirit behind this great nation is nonsectarian.

Our great American Public Schools have never taken away from any child the freedom of will, freedom of spirit or freedom of mind. That is the divine reason that Great God our King has chosen the great American Public Schools to pave the way for the new race, the new religion and the new civilization that is taking place in America.

Any mother, father or guardian who is responsible for the taking away of freedom of mind, freedom of will or freedom of spirit is the lowest criminal on this earth, because they take away from that child the God-given right to become a part of God's great plan in America for the dawn of the New Age of the world.

new and great civilization is like an American Beauty rosebud, ready to open and send its wonderful fragrance to all the world...."

In a resolution, *A World Federal Government?*, published in the same issue of the *New Age* magazine, September, 1950, Scottish Rite Masonry declared that it "recognize[s] in the United Nations a movement for the promotion of peace, harmony and better understanding among the nations of the world...."

The significance of that statement will soon become evident.

UNITED NATIONS' PLAN THE UNCED DOCUMENT

How do they plan to finally bring all nations of the world into total submission to this New World Order? The startlingly clear answer is revealed in *a document circulated privately to select officials at a closed meeting* during a state-sponsored United Nations conference in Des Moines, Iowa, on September 20, 1991. We reproduce, in their original form, what we believe are the most important segments of the six-page document.

Midnight Messenger obtained this document from an individual (a professional person and a highly respected member of their community) who was present at one of the closed meetings. He recognized the seriousness of the contents of the document, and wanted the American people to realize what is planned by the elitists. Here are some brief excerpts from the six-page, single space document:

"The time is pressing.... Given global instabilities ... the need for *firm control* of world technology, weaponry and natural resources, *is now absolutely mandatory*....

"The present vast overpopulation ... must be met in the present *by the reduction in the numbers presently existing. **This must be done by whatever means necessary**....*

"The U.N. action against Iraq [1991 Gulf War] proves conclusively that resolute action on our part can sway other leaders to go along with the necessary program...."

"In the face of mounting opposition," the document asks, is there much point in 'traipsing' around the U.S. in an effort to convince people of the "necessity of [an] Earth Charter?" The implied answer is, no! Instead, heavy duty action is called for!

OPPOSITION AND THE "BRITISH RACE PATRIOTS"

"There is a twofold opposition that must be eliminated by quick action" if their scheme is to come to fruition.

The document then lists numerous objections voiced by Algeria, Brazil and Malaysia etc. to the plans put forward by UNCED which would destroy their national sovereignty.

What is the answer to these problems as seen through the eyes of the Illuminated ones who would rule the world? The answer will prove shocking to those who have not done their homework and figured out that all the talk about establishing "democracies" worldwide and "freeing the people" is just so much pious cant. **The plan is totally White supremacist and racist in nature.** Here it is:

"This is the time to save the Anglo-Saxon race and its most glorious production, the Anglo-Saxon system of banking, insurance and trade.

"We are the loving sponsors of the great Cecil Rhodes will of 1877, in which he devoted his fortune to: **'The extension of British rule throughout the world ... [and] the ultimate recovery of the United States of America as an integral part of the British Empire....'**

"We stand by Lord Milner's Credo. We too, are 'British Race Patriots' and our patriotism is 'the speech, the tradition, the principles, the aspirations of the British Race.' Do you fear to take this stand, when this purpose can be realized? Do you not see that *failure now is to be pulled down by the billions of Lilliputians of lesser race* who care little or nothing for the Anglo-Saxon system?"

[For additional background information on Cecil Rhodes, see *Tragedy and Hope*, pp.130-133. Also, *Fourth Reich of the Rich*, pp. 74-76].

Now, to continue the UNCED document:

"THEREFORE THE FOLLOWING POLICY MUST BE IMPLEMENTED:

"A. The Security Council of the U.N., led by the Anglo-Saxon Major Nation powers, will decree that henceforth, **the Security Council will inform *all nations* that its sufferance on population *has ended*, that all nations have quotas for reduction on a yearly basis, which will be *enforced* ... by selective or total embargo of credit, items of trade including food and medicine, *or by military force, when required.*

"B. *The ... U.N. will inform all nations that outmoded notions of national sovereignty will be discarded* and that the Security Council has complete legal, military, and economic jurisdiction in any region of the world and that *this will be enforced by the Major Nations of the Security Council.*

"C. The ... U.N. will take possession of all the natural resources ... *to be used and preserved for the good of the Major Nations of the Security Council.*

"D. The ... U.N. will explain that *not* all races and peoples are equal, nor should they be. *Those races proven superior by superior achievements ought to rule the lesser nations,* caring for them *on sufferance that they cooperate* with the Security Council. Decision making, including banking, trade, currency rates, and economic development plans, *will be made in the stewardship of the Major Nations.* [How is that for White Supremacism and Racism?].

"E. All of the above constitute the New World Order, in which all nations, regions and races will cooperate with the Major Nations of the Security Council.

"The purpose of this document is to demonstrate that action delayed could well be fatal. *All could be lost if mere opposition by minor races is tolerated* and the unfortunate vacillations of our closest comrades is cause for our hesitations. *Open declaration of intent followed by decisive force is the final solution.* This must be done before any shock hits our financial markets, tarnishing our credibility and perhaps diminishing our force." **(End of document).**

"FREEDOM AND CHOICE WILL BE CONTROLLED"

Is this not exactly the kind of world foretold by Dr. Carroll Quigley, in his book *Tragedy and Hope?* Read Quigley's precise words for yourself: *The goal is "nothing less than to create a world system ... controlled in a feudalistic fashion," in which the individual's "freedom and choice will be controlled within very narrow alternatives by the fact that he will be numbered from birth and followed, as a number, through his educational training, his required military or other public service, his tax contributions, his health and medical requirements, and his final retirement and death benefits."*

Any opposition to this plan would, according to President Clinton's mentor, represent a **"revolt of the ignorant against the informed and educated ... of Siwash against Harvard"** (pp.324,979).

In October 1992, President Bush announced that he had authorized the stationing of U.N. troops in the United States. Don't be surprised if these troops, and hundreds of thousands more like them, are used in the years immediately ahead in an attempt to corral the citizens of the United States — and herd them into the Luciferian New World Order.

Such a possibility is in line with a statement made by Dr. Henry Kissinger in Evian, France, in 1991: "Today America would be outraged if U.N. troops entered Los Angeles to restore order; tomorrow they will be grateful! This is especially true if they were told that there were *an outside threat from beyond*, whether real or promulgated, that threatened our very existence. It is then that *all peoples of the world will plead to deliver them from this evil.* The one thing that every man fears is the unknown. *When presented with this scenario, individual rights will be willingly relinquished for the guarantee of their well-being granted to them by the world government.*"

NOTHING NEW

This attitude of natural superiority is nothing new; it has long been an important part of British thinking. For example: "The [British] Commonwealth is a typical section of human society including every race and level of civilization organized in one state. **In this world commonwealth** *the function of government is reserved to the European minority,* **for the unanswerable reason that for the present this portion of its citizens is alone capable of the task** — civilized states are obliged to assume control of the backward communities to protect [sic] them from exploitation by private adventurers from Europe.... (Lionel Curtis, *The Problem of the Commonwealth*, 1916).

This Anglo-Saxon white supremacist, racist philosophy is what also inspired Margaret Sanger, founder of Planned Parenthood. Sanger (1879-1966) was educated in England. In London, Sanger's mentor and lover — Havelock Ellis — was a disciple of Frances Galton, Charles Darwin's cousin and the first systematizer and popularizer of eugenics. Sanger's other radical socialist friends included H.G. Wells and George Bernard Shaw.

"She [Sanger] was thoroughly convinced that the 'inferior races' were in fact 'human weeds' and a 'menace to civilization'.... She yearned for the end of the Christian 'reign of benevolence' that the

Eugenic Socialists promised, when the 'choking human undergrowth' of 'morons and imbeciles' would be 'segregated' and 'sterilized.' Her goal was 'to create a race of thoroughbreds' by encouraging 'more children from the fit, and less from the unfit'" (George Grant, *Grand Illusion: the Legacy of Planned Parenthood*, 1988, p.91).

ONLY HOPE OF MANKIND?

In the late 1990s we are being told that the United Nations and the creation of the much ballyhooed New World Order are the only hope of mankind. It is said that in order to have true and lasting peace we must surrender our national sovereignty and become part of a one-world community.

In August 1990 President George Bush became the first American chief executive to publicly declare in favor of the New World Order. Although Bush had taken a solemn oath to "faithfully execute the office of President ... and to the best of [his] ability, preserve, protect and defend the Constitution of the United States," he in fact strove to the very best of his ability to promote the aims of the One Worlders through the United Nations. At the United Nations in New York, in January 1992, Bush stated: "It is the sacred principles enshrined in the UN Charter to which we henceforth pledge our allegiance."

Did you get that? "Sacred principles enshrined in the UN Charter"? You've got to be kidding! Anyone who has researched the matter *knows* that the UN was created by, among others, "internationalist" agents working within the Roosevelt and Truman administrations. (For details, see *Fourth Reich of the Rich*, p.145)

RELIGIOUS SYMBOLS AT
UNITED NATIONS HEADQUARTERS

It should also be noted that there are two highly significant religious symbols in the UN headquarters in New York. As one walks through the main entrance they are greeted by a large naked male statue: this is Zeus — the supreme god of the pagan pantheon. He represents Satan (a.k.a. Lucifer) "which deceives the whole world..." (*Revelation* 12:9).

Upstairs, there is a Meditation Room. This chamber has a floor plan in the shape of a truncated pyramid — the symbol of the Luciferian Illuminati; the entrance is at the base of the pyramid.

On the back wall of the Meditation Room, in geometric design, are more than one hundred occult symbols of various organizations. These include Masonry, Spiritism, and all the old fertility cults. In the center of the Meditation Room is a large black block; this is the ashlar, well known in Masonry. The rough block represents humanity being formed and polished by the use of the compass and square into a smooth, finished, even rectangular block which is fit for use in a building. This is the Masonic symbol for taking the masses of humanity and forming them into a finished block under their control — thus building their New World Order. This is a modern-day version of Adam Weishaupt's doctrine of the "perfectibility" of man by his own efforts. *Salvation by works!*

Over the top of the black block is a small single floodlight mounted in the ceiling. This sends a single shaft of light onto the black block. This symbolizes the light of the sun (or the sun god) sending its semen or seed to fertilize the earth. This, in turn, represents prosperity and success for the plan of this building through the black block — the ashlar (For photos and further documentation, see *Fourth Reich of the Rich*, pp. 159-162).

"DOUBT IT NOT"

It is obvious that the United Nations is meant to develop into a World Government — or New World Order. Top Illuminist and Sovereign Grand Commander of Scottish Rite Masonry, Southern Jurisdiction, Albert Pike (who acknowledged Lucifer as his god and told us to "doubt it not" (*Morals and Dogma*, p.321), prophesied such an event, declaring that it would be a manifestation "of the pure doctrine of Lucifer" and would result in "the destruction of Christianity and atheism, both conquered at the same time" (*Fourth Reich of the Rich*, p.71). **That**, in the final analysis, is the planned New World Order!

Chapter 10

WHAT DO YOU MEAN, CHRISTIANITY?

When an objective observer takes a long, hard look at the religious scene in the United States in the waning years of the twentieth century, they are met with a truly depressing sight. Confusion abounds; something is desperately wrong.

Increasingly, church denominations which were formerly powerful agents of stability in their communities have degenerated and disintegrated into virtual irrelevance. Many openly embrace beliefs and practices that are clearly condemned in the pages of God's word. Many of these establishments have become little more than social clubs where attendees are entertained, but never instructed in true biblical righteousness.

Religion is split into divisions and subdivisions — and into subdivisions of the subdivisions. These, all too often, are split into angry, bickering factions where infighting is the rule rather than the exception. Cults are proliferating. It is a scene that is definitely inspiring ... to the enemies of Christ!

"What a circus. Take a look at the average evangelical church and there should be no question as to why the world does not take us seriously. People falling down laughing, ministers who sound like Ringmasters announcing for *Barnum and Bailey*, brass bands playing off key as loudly as they can, hootenannies masquerading as 'praise services' and church decor that appears as if a nineteenth-century interior designer for bordellos was given carte blanche to make the place look as tacky as possible. Most every time I turn on the television to watch Christian church services I keep expecting to hear an usher yelling, as he walks up and down the aisles, 'Popcorn, Peanuts, Sacraments.'

"Instead of coming to give God what He demands, and deserves, the average evangelical comes to have his emotions pandered to. *What he wants of 'worship' is a renewal of his ego.* He demands that the service make him *feel* better about himself. The blatant narcissism of it all is simply astounding" (Monte E. Wilson, *Chalcedon Report*, May 1996, p.17).

GIMME A BREAK

Can we now be far from the time when, as part of the nauseous religious hype, scantily clad cheerleaders run onto the stage and lead the mesmerized millions who watch "Christian television" in a chant: Gimme a J...J, Gimme an E...E, Gimme an S...S, Gimme a U...U, Gimme a S...S. What does it spell? Jesus! Jesus. Rah! Rah! Rah!"

To which the writer might reply: Gimme a B, Gimme an R, Gimme an E, Gimme an A, Gimme a K. What do we have? Gimme a Break!

As the late Victor V. Bryditzki, in his hilariously funny but sadly true book, *The $elling of Je$u$ — the Confessions of a Christian Bookstore Owner*, wrote: "Mickey Mouse is growing old, Snoopy is slowly losing his touch, E.T. has finally made his phone call and gone home. Cabbage Patch dolls were harvested too fast to last. But Jeu continues to sell. In fact, Jeu is a multi-billion dollar industry, expanding into places where angels (and sober Christians) fear to tread" (p.69).

There are a number of reasons why this tragic spiritual condition exists in our nation. Particularly over the last half century we — as individuals and as a nation — have developed a strong aversion to reality and common sense. Having abandoned the habit of thinking and reasoning for ourselves — of planning ahead, of making long-term decisions for which we are personally responsible — we have, unfortunately, turned into a nation of mindless sheep, a nation obsessed with trivialities. In our mental and spiritual shallowness, we have developed an obsessive desire to escape, through fantasy, the harsh realities of the world around us. We don't want to take personal responsibility for our own lives and the decisions we make; we just want to be amused and entertained, and — without any real conscious effort on our part — be made to "feel good" and have everything turn out well in the end. Things may work out "happily ever after" in fairy tales — but very seldom in real life!

When we review the documentation presented in the early chapters of this book, we find that **nothing** has really changed throughout mankind's six thousand year history on planet earth. It seems that man is destined to live — and interminably relive — his own mistakes and follies without ever grasping the truth about his own hideous predicament. A brief comparison between Ancient Rome and modern America (see *Descent Into Slavery?* pp.1-5) proves that point beyond a shadow of doubt.

A VITAL DIFFERENCE

At the end of the twentieth century the American religious scene — like so many other aspects of our society — resembles a disaster area; spiritual wreckage is strewn from coast to coast. Countless millions of churchgoers are languishing in spiritual poverty; most are dying of spiritual malnutrition.

The "church" scene in America today may be divided into three sections: Churchianity, Religion, and Biblical Christianity. The first is mostly made up of the staid old established churches which have long since abandoned the concept of an Almighty Creator God who is actively concerned about — and involved in — the daily lives of their members. Many decades ago, they jettisoned their once professed belief in the sovereignty of God, the Lordship of Jesus Christ, and the inerrancy of scripture.

Churchianity consists of dull, boring, meaningless ritual, and mindless ceremony — all wrapped up in dead doctrine. Having nothing meaningful, challenging, inspirational, or productive to offer society at large, the activities of such institutions are — in the final analysis — totally irrelevant and thus non-productive in today's high-tech world.

RELIGION

What is termed "Religion" by this author is basically what Monte Wilson was referring to in his observations quoted earlier in this chapter. It primarily manifests itself in frenzied outbreaks of what is perceived to be "spiritual" activity. By its adherents, this is generally believed to consist of activities that focus people's attention on individuals who are feverishly engaged in such "spiritual" exercises. These activities embody, but are not limited to, "speaking in tongues," loud singing and strenuous arm waving, thunderous shouting, lots of cries of "alleluia" and "praise the Lord," and the repetition of words and phrases that are perceived to be "spiritual." The more fervor, presumably the greater one's "spirituality."

Unfortunately, such people are generally consumed with an overwhelming pride and vanity. Despite their alleged spirituality, presumed righteousness, and syrupy "love," their numbers are mainly comprised of very empty people who are usually so busy talking, gyrating, smugly "counseling" others, shouting, or otherwise making senseless noises that they have no time to listen to God's word. *Empty cans always make the most noise!*

Their religion is based on sentiment and "feelings," instead of biblical knowledge, understanding, convictions, and the working of the Holy Spirit. They substitute emotional sensations and feelings for reality and spiritual substance. They attempt to generate through the emotions — and through their self-generated "spiritual" fervor — what only God can do through the power of his Holy Spirit. They possibly believe that if they fake it for long enough they will somehow, miraculously, make it. But it doesn't work that way; it never has, and it never will!

When their "hootenannies masquerading as 'praise' services" are over — and they return to the real world — nothing has really changed. Their vanities and egos may have been massaged, but their emotional conflicts and very real spiritual emptiness still remain. The resultant frustration is devastating; it leads to what has been rightly termed spiritual burnout.

"SPIRITUAL LEADERS"

In Religion, pastors and other "spiritual leaders" are frequently little more than posturing jackasses — prancing, dancing clowns — whose glib tongues and slick presentations beguile many honest people who are seeking for something — they know not what — to fill the gaping spiritual void that exists in their lives.

The innumerable sex and other scandals (Bakker, Swaggert, Tilden, Popov, Hinn, Larson, et. al.) that have sprung from such religious activities bear mute testimony to the fact that — although they may outwardly appear to talk the talk — they most certainly don't walk the walk. As the Lord Jesus Christ stated so clearly: "*Wherefore by their fruits shall you know them*" (*Matthew* 7:20)

WANTED: NEW PASTOR

Complacent community church looking for non-progressive, pious, middle-aged pastor. (If unavailable, a younger, bright-eyed, bouncy "social director" type would be acceptable). Must be dedicated to basic irrelevencies and to preserving the status quo, not rocking the boat — and not dealing with reality. Political correctness is of utmost importance. Must be subservient to monetary donors. Wet-nursing skills and a proven ability to referee "sand-box" squabbles are prerequisites.

Most sermons must be bland — but entertaining — and void of any spiritual and intellectual stimulants. Hell fire and guilt trips are, on occasion, permissible (and even desirable). Strict and mindless adherence to traditional orthodoxy is mandatory. A moderate sense of humor is acceptable, as long as, even in jest, no word of truth is spoken.

Additionally, sermons must be scripted in utter simplicity — geared to an IQ level of 25 or less. They must be designed to produce a warm fuzzy, fluffy, frothy sense of euphoria sufficient to carry the parishoners blissfully through the week in a buffering bubble of non-reality.

Salary is negotiable depending upon degree of conformity.

Chapter 11

THE GREAT AMERICAN PASTOR DISASTER

These are times that truly try men's souls. These are also times that cry out for tried and true leaders — leaders who are not for sale; leaders who are honest, sound from center to circumference; leaders who will tell the truth and look the world right in the eye; leaders in whom the courage of everlasting life runs deep, still and strong — leaders who know their message and tell it — straight and unflinchingly!

The United States today — as never before in its history — needs leaders who will "cry aloud and spare not" and lay the truth before the people in no uncertain terms. But where are these leaders — these blowers of the trumpets — in the late 1990s when they are needed most?

The few such leaders who do exist in the political arena are extremely few and far between. They are an almost extinct species —

their true worth recognized by only a pitifully small remnant who have been granted "eyes to see and ears to hear."

On the religious front things are even worse; here we have a scene that is even more sickening and depressing. Never before in our nation's history has the religious scene been more fragmented, chaotic and confused — and in such pathetic disarray as in these tumultuous 90s. A frightening number of pulpits across the land are occupied by semi-literate wimps with little or no true biblical education — and even less understanding. These preachers have been mass-produced by religious seminaries (perhaps religious cemeteries would be a more apt description, for biblical truth is usually deeply buried in these institutions!). These assembly line pastors have been mass-produced through a religious seminary system that has long-since rejected the Sovereignty of God, the Lordship of Jesus Christ and the inerrancy of Scripture as its foundation. For the most part, these cookie cutter preachers have graduated from seminary along a very short, narrow and circuitous route through their Bibles. As lobotomized seminarians they have not been trained to "prove all things" as instructed in Holy Writ (*I Thessalonians* 5:21). Due to a lack of thorough training and a truly biblical education, they emerge from these institutions incapable of rational thought and logical deduction — and are thus ill-equipped to deal with the problems they and their unfortunate future congregations encounter in their every day lives.

Once the fantasy bubble bursts — and they come face-to-face with the way things really are — many try to "fake it till they make it." They "talk the talk" but deep down inside their empty, frustrated hearts they know that they are not "walking the walk."

This, in turn, leads to a massive identity crisis and ultimate spiritual burnout. Many quit the ministry or turn their churches into what amounts to little more than social clubs, whose inward convictions are at hopeless variance with their outward profession.

"PROVING" THEMSELVES

The majority of the more naturally gifted of these seminary graduates, refusing to acknowledge their own lack of spiritual training and preparedness, feel a compelling need to "prove" themselves. Lacking — either through miseducation or a lack of calling — a true biblical perspective and spiritual understanding of what Christianity is really all about, they set about developing mega churches that will be highly respected in their local areas and "honored" by society at large. In their quest for "acceptance" by the world, they constantly compromise and become increasingly "broadminded" in their worldview; the Bible becomes only of secondary importance — if that!

"I NEVER KNEW YOU"

In *Matthew* 7, Jesus stated: "**Not everyone** that **says** unto me, Lord, Lord, shall enter into the kingdom of heaven, but he that **does** the will of my Father which is in heaven.

"Many will **say** to me in that day, Lord, Lord, have we not prophesied in your name? and in your name have cast out devils? and in your name done many wonderful works.

"Then will I profess unto them, **I never knew you**; depart from me, you that work iniquity" (*Matthew* 7:21-23).

Notice carefully what Jesus said. Outwardly, these people appear to be deeply spiritual. They use what appear to many to be all the right words; they go through what appear to many to be all the right religious routines. But, despite what other religious people around them might have thought, they were, in fact, workers of iniquity.

But how could this possibly be? Jesus answers: "Why call you me, Lord, Lord, **and do not the things which I say?**" *Luke* 6:46). The religious people were talking the talk, but they weren't walking the walk!

Again, Jesus explains by stating a number of profound truths. He, alone, is "the way, the truth, and the light" (*John* 14:6)."*I am the door of the sheep.... by me if any man enter in, he shall be saved, and shall go in and out, and find pasture*" (*John* 10:7,9). In addition, Jesus declared that: "No man can come to me, except the Father which has sent me draw[4] him" (*John* 6:44).

With that background in mind, we can now clearly understand — **from scripture** — the true meaning of Jesus' words. These workers of "iniquity" (lawlessness) attempt to get into the kingdom their own way — by doing their own thing. They aren't interested in repenting, studying, changing, growing, overcoming. Most are undoubtedly doing what seemed "right in [their] own eyes." The Lord, however, weighs the spirits (*Proverbs* 12:15). The Lord also "ponders their

---

[4] The definition of draw here is "to drag" against one's will (*Strong's* #1670).

hearts" (*Proverbs* 21:1). In the Lord's eyes, all their perceived righteousness and spirituality are "as filthy rags" (*Isaiah* 64:6).

Jesus further clarifies the situation: "Verily, verily, I say unto you, He that enters not **by the door** into the sheepfold, but **climbs up some other way**, the same is a thief and a robber" (*John* 10:1). Obviously, a thief and a robber is also a "worker of iniquity."

They are "blind leaders of the blind — individuals who have no true godliness and even less character. And if the blind lead the blind, both shall fall into the ditch" (*Matthew* 15:14). Hence their condemnation by Jesus.

"His watchmen are blind: they are all ignorant, they are all dumb dogs, they cannot bark; sleeping, lying down, loving to slumber. Yes, they are greedy dogs which can never have enough, and they are **shepherds** that cannot understand: they all look to their own way, every one for his gain..." (*Isaiah* 56:10-11).

"ITCHING EARS"

Now, notice carefully a couple of massive problems that the Apostle Paul, under the inspiration of the Holy Spirit, said would characterize the religious scene at the end time. He admonished true pastors to, "Preach the word; be instant in season, out of season; reprove, rebuke, exhort with all long suffering and doctrine."

Why was he so concerned? "**For** the time will come when they will **not** endure sound doctrine; but **after their own lusts** they shall **heap** to themselves teachers having itching ears;

"**And they shall turn away their ears from the truth, and shall be turned unto fables**" (*II Timothy* 4:

This, of course, produces a situation in which people are so enmeshed in makebelieve that they have no interest in "earnestly contend[ing] for the faith once delivered to the saints" (*Jude* 1:3). They just want to be amused, entertained (have their "itching ears" tickled), and made to "feel good."

When these pastoral exercises in futility collapse (and they always do!), they feel impelled to make their religion "more attractive" to the public so that the people — *and their money* — will keep pouring in. This inevitably leads to still more bizarre efforts — more trite gimmicks, games, and exercises in futility — to keep their congregations busy, psyched-up, and coming back week after week. Their's is a very temporary triumph of trivia over substance, of fantasy over reality.

The end result is always the same — anger, frustration, anguish, and spiritual burnout.

"FAITH ONCE DELIVERED"?

Another vital question needs to be asked — and answered: Why do these religious leaders feel the need to make their religion "more attractive" to the public? If they are, in fact, proclaiming the truth "which was **once** delivered to the saints" (*Jude* 1:3) by the Perfectly Righteous Sovereign God, how would it be possible to make that truth "more attractive"?

Obviously, one cannot improve on divine perfection. Common sense dictates, therefore, that the original premise upon which their ministry was based must have been in error. This is further emphasized by the fact that not only are there few positive, constructive, life-changing, society-changing results being produced by modern religion. Not only so, but religion's lack of dedication to true biblical righteousness is a major factor in the ongoing disintegration of American society.

"SALT OF THE EARTH"

In the New Testament, true Christians are called "**the** salt of the earth" (*Matthew* 5:13). True Christians are **the** major preserving agent in a sound, law-abiding society in much the same way as salt is a natural preservative. But we are told in the same verse that "if the salt has lost its savor ... it is thenceforth good for nothing, but to be cast out, and to be trodden under foot of men."

As that is true, there is yet another possibility regarding the many religious leaders: "[I]f he that comes preaches **another Jesus**, whom we have **not** preached, or if you receive **another spirit**, which we have **not** received, or **another gospel**, which you have **not** accepted, you might well bear with him" (*II Corinthians* 11:4).

Staggering as it may appear, unbelievable as it may sound, is it remotely possible that modern religion may, in fact, be preaching another "Jesus," have another "spirit," and be proclaiming another "gospel"?

If a church or a pastor promises you a delicious and nutritious spiritual "steak" but produces only what sounds like the sizzle of a spiritual steak — but never any real spiritual meat — their assembly may be little more than a spiritual grave yard; such places are filled with the spiritually dead, or dysfunctional individuals who are dying of spiritual malnutrition.

These are among the signs that they may, in fact, be dealing with another "Jesus," another "spirit," and another "gospel." By their fruit shall you know them!

DISTURBING PARALLELS

There are many disturbing parallels between what is happening on the religious scene today and conditions that existed just before Judah was conquered and went into the Babylonian Captivity some 600 years before Christ. At that time, the prophet Jeremiah cried out in condemnation of the religious leaders. In chapter 23, we read:

"Woe be unto the pastors that destroy and scatter the sheep of my pasture! says the Lord....

"You have scattered my flock, and driven them away, and have not visited them: behold, I will visit upon you the evil of your doings, says the Lord" (vs.1,2).

"My heart is broken within me because of the prophets; all my bones shake; I am like a drunken man and like a man whom wine has overcome, because of the Lord, and because of the words of his holiness.

"For the land is full of adulteries; for because of swearing the land mourns; the pleasant places of the wilderness are dried up, and their course is evil, and their force is not right.

"For both prophet and priest are profane" (vs.9-11).

"I have seen also in the prophets of Jerusalem a horrible thing: they commit adultery, and walk in lies: they strengthen also the hands of evil doers, that none does return from his wickedness; they are all unto me as Sodom, and the inhabitants thereof as Gomorrah" (v.14).

"The Lord of hosts says, Don't listen to the words of the prophets that prophesy to you: they make you vain: they speak a vision of their own heart, and not out of the mouth of the Lord" (v.16).

"I have not sent these prophets, yet they ran: I have not spoken to them, yet they prophesied" (v.21)

They "have perverted the words of the Living God, of the Lord of Hosts our God" (v.36).

"And I will bring an everlasting reproach upon you, and a perpetual shame, which shall not be forgotten."

In the New Testament, Christ warned us: "Beware of false prophets [and pastors], which come to you in sheep's clothing, but inwardly they are ravening wolves" (*Matthew* 7:15). Webster's 1828 dictionary defines "ravening" as "preying with rapacity, voraciously devouring; as a ravening wolf."

As you are as "sheep in the midst of wolves, be you therefore wise as serpents, and harmless as doves" (*Matthew* 10:16).

It may be time to move on.

CREATIONS OF BABYLON

Despite the strong biblical admonition for Christians to "come out" of the Babylonian system that has historically dominated the world scene (*Revelation* 18:4) — and in direct violation of Christ's command that his followers "be ... not equally yoked together with unbelievers: for what fellowship has righteousness with unrighteousness? and what communion has light with darkness?" (*II Corinthians* 6:14) — these self-appointed "spiritual leaders" have gone out of their way to commit spiritual fornication with the world's system. "You adulterers and adulteresses, know you not that the friendship of the world is enmity with God? whosoever therefore will be a friend of the world is the enemy of God" (*James* 4:4). Being unable to believe and acknowledge Christ's promise that he would build **his** church (**his** body) as **he** sees fit, these ministers go to the secular, worldly state authorities, asking for permission to build their own churches by the state's grace and authority.

By going to the state and by seeking its permission to exist, these mega pastors and would-be mega pastors have in fact been instrumental in bringing into being commercial entities — complete with 501 (C)(3) "tax exempt" status — that are created by the state and thus under its control. **The creator always has authority over its creation!**

By voluntarily contracting with the government — and thus acknowledging the state as its creator and protector instead of the Lord Jesus Christ — all such American church organizations deny the Lordship of Christ and thus give up their First Amendment protection guaranteed by the United States Constitution. They become creations and property of the state.

In the final analysis, states do not create churches: states create commercial corporations. All commercial corporations (the only type that exist in the U.S) are creatures of commerce. Their 501 (C)(3) status is a privilege granted by the creator state; it can be revoked at any time, thus making these commercial organizations totally dependent upon the will of the state authorities. *Caesar is their lord, their boss — not the Lord Jesus Christ.*

DEFECTIVE EDUCATIONAL SYSTEM

Most pastors are products of a highly defective religious "educational" system and are extraordinarily uninformed in many important areas.

With a pinch of biblical knowledge and a modicum of logical deduction, even the least literate of these seminary graduates should be able to figure out the dangers of seeking to become a state-created corporation.

One would think that after four or more years in "Bible college" (where, incidentally, very little true Bible is taught) they would somehow have stumbled across the biblical commands against having close associations (contractual agreements, etc.) with the governments of this world (See *Joshua* 9; *II Corinthians* 6:14; *Revelation* 18:4 and *James* 4:4).

CORPORATION?

One would also think that they would have somehow discovered that the church founded by Jesus Christ is already a corporation — Jesus Christ himself having incorporated it nearly 2,000 years ago. The word incorporate is from the Latin, using the root word "corp" or "corpus" meaning body (*I Corinthians* 12:12). Scripture clearly states that Christ is "the head of the church: and he is the savior of the body" [his corporation] (*Ephesians* 5:23).

Jesus Christ is the head of his church, the body (corporation) of Christ. There is no other head intended. He alone is King of kings, and Lord of lords. If there is **any** other head above him, **any** other entity to whom we must bow or to whom we must give allegiance before Jesus Christ, then that entity is the head over Christ.

The true church or body of Christ is a spiritual organ**ism**, not a state-created organ**ization**. The Lord Jesus Christ has redeemed *his* people by **his** own blood (*Colossians* 1:14). *They* are saved by **his** life (*Romans* 5:10). Christ **in** them is their only "hope of glory" (*Colossians* 1:27). In Christ there is "no condemnation" for we are "passed from death unto life" (*Romans* 8:1; *John* 5:24).

Jesus Christ as Redeemer, Savior and Lord is "**the** Way, **the** Truth, and **the** Life" (*John* 14:6). It should be obvious, even to a biblically-illiterate seminary graduate, that as Christ is **the** Way, **the** Truth, and **the** Life, there cannot be *any* other right way of doing things apart from **his** way. *Everything* else is futile. These are the ABCs of Christian reality.

GOD'S COMMAND?

What is God's command to those few of his true servants who may be thus ensnared with the Babylonian System? "Be you not enequally yoked together with unbelievers: for what fellowship has righteousness with unrighteousness? and what communion has light with darkness? ... Come out from among them and be you separate, says the Lord" (*II Corinthians* 6:14,17). Those who are Christ's true sheep will hear his voice and follow him (*John* 10:27).

Incidentally, contrary to popular misconceptions and virtually without exception, most true pastors of God have been trained the biblical way — through one-on-one relationships with older pastors who have, from the beginning, been trained in a similar manner. The pattern is clearly laid out in *II Timothy* 2:1,2. Religious seminaries are unknown in scripture.

RELIGIOUS DEVASTATION

What have been the fruits borne by this Great Pastor Disaster?

As mentioned earlier, French historian Alexis De Tocqueville (1805-1859) marveled at the results produced by the American Republic. He sought to explain what he saw by almost every means, but was unable to do so. He later realized that it was not until he went into the churches of the land (which he testified were "aflame with righteousness") that he began to understand the secret behind America's spectacular success. As Benjamin Franklin had pointed out earlier in his book, *Nation Under God*, the true gospel of the Sovereignty of God and the Lordship of Jesus Christ had a "wonderful" and "extraordinary influence" on early America; it produced churches that were "aflame with righteousness."

Shortly after the time of De Tocqueville's visit to America (1831-1832) a number of deadly viruses were injected into the American religious community. These were the false teachings that sprang from the "dreams" and "visions" (allegedly from God) experienced by a young Scottish girl named Margaret Macdonald in the spring of 1830. They concerned an alleged secret Pre-Trib Rapture of the Saints and the establishment of a physical "Kingdom of God" on earth. Although Macdonald shunned publicity, her unscriptural and highly-destructive teachings were eagerly seized upon by John Darby, the organizer and promoter of the Plymouth Brethren. Darby spent much time with Macdonald, learning the details of her "spiritual" experiences. He then set out to exploit the "new revelations" to the fullest.

When — during a trip to the United States in 1836 — Darby's unscriptural teachings were rejected by the religious community as a whole he condemned them for their lack of "spirituality." However, some 30 years later — when his heresies began to take root in the churches of America — he rejoiced in the belief that "the Lord is working in the States." As they say in show business, the rest is history — and downhill all the way!

As a result of a lack of biblical discernment, belief in the demonically-inspired hallucinations of a young Scottish girl instead of the plain word of the Sovereign God, and the popularization of these spiritual heresies by John Darby, Edward Irving, C.I. Scofield and a long list of more recent preachers such as the many-times-married Hal Lindsey, the religious community in America has been ravaged, and laid virtually desolate!

CHURCHIANITY HAS FORSAKEN TRUE DOCTRINE

Modern churchianity has forsaken the true doctrine of the Bible which clearly states the condition of man: "There is none righteous, no, not one. There is none that understands, there is none that seeks after God" (*Romans* 3:10,11). If none seeks, how do any come to believe in Christ? "No man can come to me, except the father which has sent me draw him" (*John* 6:44). What has been given unto us to believe? "For God so loved the world, that he gave his only begotten Son, that whosoever believes in him should not perish but have everlasting life" (*John* 3:16). What is "the world" that God loves? Is it all men in general? "All that the father gives me shall come to me; and him that comes to me I shall in no wise cast out" (*John* 6:37).

And who are all that the father has given to Christ? "According as he has chosen us in him before the foundation of the world, that we should be holy and without blame before him in love: Having predestinated us unto the adoption of children by Jesus Christ to himself, according to the good pleasure of his will.... In whom we have also obtained an inheritance, being predestinated according to the purpose of him who works all things according after the counsel of his own will" (*Ephesians* 1:4,5,11). And who is Christ? "For unto us a child is born, unto us a son is given: and the government shall be upon his shoulder: and his name shall be called Wonderful Counsellor, The mighty God, The everlasting Father, The Prince of Peace" (*Isaiah* 9:6).

INDOCTRINATION CENTERS
FOR THE NEW WORLD ORDER

Contrary to clear Bible teaching, most modern churches have forsaken the responsibility of the everyday education of children in the ways of the Lord (*Proverbs* 22:6). All too frequently, they have handed that responsibility over to the Humanistic, God-denying, Christ-defying government-controlled "public schools" which teach that the State is god. Incredible? Yes, but true! In their disobedience, they have lost the battle for the minds of their children by default!

Government schools have only one purpose. Contrary to popular belief, that purpose is not to educate our nation's youth in the truest sense of the word; the main purpose of government schools is to indoctrinate their unwitting, unsuspecting charges in the anti-American, anti-Christian tenets of the Humanist religion — the concept that there is no such thing as right and wrong, that there are no absolutes and that man, alone, is responsible for developing his own belief systems.

They also teach that collective man — in the form of the State— is god and the sole arbiter of what is acceptable in society, and that the State god will take care of their every need from the cradle to the grave.

With a minimal amount of mental exertion, it should be clear to everyone capable of logical deduction that such a system would both strongly resent and rigorously resist any "competition" from the God of the Bible. Should the reader doubt the veracity of that statement they should pay particular attention to the words of a few top "experts" in the field of what is generally accepted as Education: Ashley Montagu stated in a lecture to an Education convention held in California in 1970 that, "The American family structure produces mentally ill children." Paul Brandwein declared that, "Any child who believes in God is mentally ill" (*Social Sciences*, Harcourt Brace, 1970, p.10).

At another convention on Education, Dr. Pierce of Harvard pontificated: "Every child in America who enters school at the age of five is mentally ill, because he comes to school with allegiance toward our elected officials, toward our founding fathers, toward our institutions [churches included], toward the preservation of this form of government ... patriotism, nationalism, sovereignty.... *All these prove the child is sick, because the truly well individual is one who has rejected all of these things and is what I call the true international child of the future.*" In plain terms, the government-controlled education system — run by self-admitted change agents — is specifically designed to prepare our nation's youth (through indoctrination) to be good little Globalists and totally dependant upon the Babylonian One World System.

Don't be deceived — this is **educational reality 101** in the United States today. Why, then, do so many apparently sane, logical churchgoers so willingly grant permission to the State to marinate their children's minds in a cesspool of Babylonian iniquity and then expect them to emerge at age 18 smelling like roses? In some cases (thank God!) this would appear, in some miraculous way, to happen — but the apparently terminal insanity rampant in our society is a strong indication that government-run public schools cause severe or even irreparable brain damage. Perhaps the best proof of this fact can be found sitting in the church pews of our land. The totally-overwhelming majority of these brain-dead clones who supposedly worship and serve the Almighty, Creator God of heaven and earth — and who also supposedly acknowledge Jesus Christ as their Redeemer, Savior and Lord — are usually among the first in line to sign up for the all "benefits" allegedly offered by the Babylonian System.

EMBARRASSED?

It was said years ago that many churchgoers were so "heavenly minded that they were of no earthly use." In the late 1990s it is probably more accurate to say that most churchgoers are so "earthly minded that they are of no heavenly use." It is a simple fact that most churchgoers are embarrassed by the real Jesus Christ — the Christ of the Bible. In their syrupy "love" and sanctimonious self-righteousness, many are even willing to forgive Jesus for not having the same doctrine as they do.

No wonder so many of these double-minded churchgoers are "unstable in all [their] ways" (*James* 1:8) — suffering from a vast array of psychological aberrations that are diametrically opposite to the sound minded, more abundant life (not to mention the "peace of God which passes all understanding") that are promised in Scripture (*II Timothy* 1:7; *John* 10:10; *Philippians* 4:7). Furthermore, they are certainly not "new creatures" whose "inward man is renewed day by day" and who are "more than conquerors" through Jesus Christ (*Galatians* 6:15; *II Corinthians* 4:16; *Romans* 8:37). Due to a number of factors, such as those discussed above, these basic fruits of Biblical Christianity are virtually nonexistent amongst today's churchgoers. They don't know — and don't even want to know — the truth; as a result, they have not been made spiritually free as promised by Christ (*John* 8:32).

WHAT DOES THE FUTURE HOLD?

As the two witnesses (the Church and the Written Word) are to all intents and purposes now dead and "lying in the streets," being rejoiced over by the enemies of God, there is little real opposition to the continued formation of the New World Order. But, as we shall see in a later chapter, that will not be true for long.

Prophecy indicates that when the Luciferian Illuminati is within inches of achieving its diabolical goal of One World Government, Almighty God will release a worldwide Christian witness of unprecedented proportions. When that witness has been completed, God will take his Church and his Word away from the earth in preparation for his final judgment (*Revelation* 11:7-15).

Prophecy also indicates that the nations of the New World Order will unite and give their power to the world ruler. Let scripture have the final word: "These shall make war with the Lamb [Jesus Christ, *John* 1:36], and the Lamb shall overcome them: for he is Lord of lords, and King of kings: and they that are with him are called, and chosen, and faithful" (*Revelation* 17:14).

And all the saints shall say, Amen!

CHAPTER 12

ABRAHAMIC COVENANT

This chapter — perhaps more than any other in this book — has the potential to make many readers upset, even incensed. The author understands such a possible reaction; he reacted in a similar manner when initially confronted with the same information.

After all, hadn't he been a "Bible student" for quarter of a century? Wasn't he able to quote literally hundreds of scriptures verbatim? Hadn't he poured tens of thousands of dollars into the spreading of "the gospel" and the news of "the glorious reign of Jesus Christ from Jerusalem during the Millennium"?

How could he possibly be wrong? After all, weren't all the great radio and television evangelists — men who could fill huge auditoriums, even giant stadiums in virtually every city in the nation — basically teaching what he believed to be the truth. Also, hadn't Hal Lindsey sold more than 30,000,000 copies of a book proclaiming the same "truths." Wasn't it "impossible for all these great men of God" to be in error?

For decades, this "gospel of the kingdom" had been preached worldwide; the religious community as a whole accepted what was said without question; this writer certainly did! With countless millions of other churchgoers, he had never even thought about the possibility that some of his basic assumptions could be deeply rooted in error. How could they be? They were "in the Bible," weren't they?

But were they really "in the Bible"? That was the question!

THEOLOGICAL HAND GRENADE

In the spring of 1978, we sponsored a weekend educational seminar by Dr. Stuart Crane in the Los Angeles area. Having picked up Dr. Crane at LAX — and with three others in the car — we were heading toward the hotel at which the seminar was to be held. Our conversation ranged over a variety of topics — politics, history, economics, and education, before focusing on the Bible.

One of the other passengers expressed delight in the belief that Christ would soon be returning to earth to set up his millennial kingdom and thus end all earth's problems. Suddenly, without warning, Dr. Crane — who was seated in front next the driver — calmly tossed a theological hand grenade over his shoulder: "You know," he said, "that's not what your Bible teaches."

I can't remember where or how the conversation went for the rest of our journey to the hotel. I do, however, clearly remember thinking that although Dr. Crane was probably right on most of the topics he expounded in his seminars, he was obviously in error on this one point.

This writer must frankly admit that in 1978 he was deeply bogged down in a false prophetic system that is still erroneously believed by probably 90-95 percent of churchgoers today; it took him about eight years to break totally free from the false premises he had wholeheartedly embraced for more than 25 years.

WORLD EVENTS AND "PROPHECY"

About the same time another, parallel "problem" arose that was of considerable concern. This writer looked at events unfolding on the world scene and realized that many of the "prophecies" he believed to be "in the Bible" were not falling into place as anticipated. However, the events forecast in another book known as *The Protocols* — a document dating from at least the early part of the twentieth century and that had been reprinted in his first book, *Fourth Reich of the Rich* — were in fact falling into place exactly as outlined.

How could this be? Were the prophecies contained in God's word in error, but the forecasts made in *The Protocols* true? Impossible!

As scriptures states, "God forbid: yes, let God be true but every man a liar" *(Romans 3:4). There had to be another explanation.*

CHECKING BIBLICAL PREMISES

This realization drove him to go back and check all the biblical premises upon which he had built his world view. What resulted was a recognition of the fact that he had previously mistakenly — but very sincerely — accepted, without first thoroughly checking their source, a number of premises that had been presented to him by certain preachers and organizations many years before.

This, in turn, led to an understanding of the fact that when one starts off with a false premise everything built on that erroneous assumption must — of necessity — be out of alignment with the truth. It will ultimately collapse and come to nothing.

Further research led to a much closer examination of basic Bible doctrine, and the covenant upon which the Christian faith is based — i.e. the Abrahamic Covenant.

THE ABRAHAMIC COVENANT

Let us now examine — *exclusively from the pages of God's word* — this vital covenant. If we are to be honest, we must not assume anything or read into any passage of scripture what is not there. Neither must we accept, without clear biblical proof, something we may have read or heard somewhere in the past. Let the Bible interpret itself. Let the Bible itself answer those questions that arise from the study of its pages.

The Covenant that the Almighty Creator God made with Abraham is found in Genesis, the first book of the Bible: "Now the LORD had said unto Abram, Get **out of** your country, and **from** your kindred, and **from** your father's house, unto a land that I will show you:

"And I will make of you a great nation, and I will bless you, and make your name great; and you shall be a blessing.

"And I will bless them that bless you, and curse him that curses you; and in you shall all families of the earth be blessed" (*Genesis* 12:1-3).

In the next chapter the Bible states: "And the Lord said unto Abram, after that Lot was separated from him, Lift up now your eyes, and look from the place where you are northward, and southward, and eastward, and westward.

ABRAHAMIC COVENANT

"For all **the land which you see, to you will I gave it**, and to your seed for ever.

"And **I will make your seed as the dust of the earth**: so that if a man can number the dust of the earth, then shall your seed also be numbered.

"Arise, walk through the land in the length of it and in the breadth of it; for I will give it unto you" (*Genesis* 13:14-17).

DEUTERONOMY 28

As is true with any covenant or contract, the covenant God made with Abraham had conditions — certain acts that had to be performed by both parties. As time went by, God gave the descendants of Abraham, now known as Israel, certain laws, statutes and judgments. He commanded that they "keep and do them with all [their] heart and with all [their] soul." He directed them to "walk in his ways, and to keep his statutes and commandments" so that they might be a "peculiar people" and be "high above all nations" (*Deuteronomy* 26:16-17).

Two chapters later, God got more specific. Here we find the "blessings" that God stated would come upon Israel as a result of their obedience — and the "cursings" that would result in the event of rebellion and disobedience. If they diligently listened to and obeyed all his commandments, God would set them "on high above all nations of the earth." Blessings would overtake them in their personal lives, and in their marriages, families and cities. Their crops would be superabundant, their storehouses overflowing. The Lord would make them "plenteous in goods, in the fruit of their body, and in the fruit of their cattle, and in the fruit of their ground." He would bless everything they set their hands to do, and cause their enemies to flee before them seven ways.

They would be able to lend to many nations, and would never have to borrow. God would make them "the head and not the tail."

All they had to do to receive everything their hearts could desire was to obey God's command that "you shall not go aside from any of the words which I command you this day, to the right hand or to the left, to go after other gods to serve them" (*Deuteronomy* 28:1-14).

BUT ... there was a stern warning in case of disobedience. Starting with verse 15, we read: "**But** it **shall** come to pass, **if** you will **not** listen to the voice of the Lord your God, to observe to **do** all **his** commandments and statutes ... **that all these curses shall come upon you, and overtake you.**" The verses that follow contain a long list of afflictions that would — in the event of their disobedience — affect and devastate every aspect of their lives.

If they continued in such rebellion, God said, the time would come when, "You shall eat the fruit of your own body, the flesh of your sons and of your daughters, which the Lord your God has given you, in the siege and in the straitness, with which your enemies shall distress you" (*Deuteronomy* 28:53).

DID GOD KEEP HIS WORD?

Did God really mean what he said in all the verses quoted above? The answer comes from other passages found elsewhere in God's word: "The Lord God of Israel ... who **keepeth covenant** and mercy **with your servants that walk before you with all their heart**" (*I Kings* 8:23)

"The Lord God of Israel ... **which keepeth covenant**, and showeth mercy unto your servants, **that walk before you with all their hearts**" (*II Chronicles* 6:14)

"The Lord God of heaven ... **that keepeth covenant** and mercy for **them that love him and observe his commandments**" (*Nehemiah* 1:5)

"My covenant will I not break, nor alter the thing that has gone out of my lips" (*Psalm* 89:34)

God was unreservedly (100 percent) committed. He would never break the blood-sealed covenant he made with Abram. Therefore, as it is "impossible for God to lie" (*Hebrews* 6:18), it must be shown **from scripture** when and how each of these covenant promises were fulfilled.

WERE GOD'S PROMISES
TO ABRAHAM FULFILLED?

"And the Lord gave Israel **all** the land which he sware to give unto their fathers; **and they possessed it, and dwelt therein.**

"The Lord gave them rest round about, according to all that he sware unto their father: and there stood not a man of all their enemies before them; and the Lord delivered **all** their enemies into their hands.

"**There failed not** ought **of any** good thing which the Lord had spoken unto the house of Israel; **all came to pass**" (*Joshua* 21:43-45).

"So David gathered **all Israel** together, from Shihor of Egypt even unto the entering of Hemath [all the land from the Nile to the Euphrates that God had promised them], to bring the ark of God from Kirjathjeaim" (*I Chronicles* 13:13)

"Blessed be the Lord, that **has** given rest unto his people Israel, according to **all** that he promised: there has **not** failed **one word** of **all** his good promise, which he promised by the hand of Moses his servant" (*I Kings* 8:56)

"And at that time Solomon held a feast, and all Israel with him, a great congregation **from the entering in of Hamath unto the river of Egypt**, before the Lord our God...." (*I Kings* 8:65)

"**You** art the Lord the God, who **chose** Abram, and brought him forth out of Ur of the Chaldees, and **gave** him the name of Abraham;

"And **found his heart to be faithful before you**, and made a covenant with him to give the land of the Canaanites, the Hittites, the Amorites, the Perizzites. and the Jebusites, and the Girgashites, to give it, I say, to his seed, **and have performed your words; for you are righteous**.... (*Nehemiah* 9:7-8).

The Bible clearly shows that God gave Abraham the land as he promised. But how about God's promise to make Abraham's descendants....

"AS THE DUST OF THE EARTH" AND "AS THE STARS OF HEAVEN"?

"And Solomon said unto God.... You **have** made me a king over **a people like the dust of the earth in multitude**" (*II Chronicles* 1:8,9)

"Therefore sprang there even of one [Abraham], and him as good as dead, **so many as the stars of the sky in multitude, and as the sand that is upon the sea shore innumerable**" (*Hebrews* 11:12).

"Their children also **multiplied you as the stars of heaven, and brought them into the land, concerning which you had promised to their fathers**, that they should go in to possess it.

"**So the children went in and possessed the land**, and they subdued before them the inhabitants of the land, the Canaanites, and gave them into their hands, with their kings, and the people of the land, they might do to them as they would" (*Nehemiah* 9:7,8,23,24).

As time went by, the Israelites weren't content to have God rule over them through the judges he had set up. When some of Samuel's sons who had been appointed judges became corrupted and "perverted judgment," the people demanded a king; they wanted to be just like all the other nations. As God said to Samuel, "[T]hey have not rejected you, but **they have rejected me that I should reign over them**" (*I Samuel* 8:1-9). Unwilling to let God straighten out the problem in his own way — and in his own time — the people took matters into their own hands.

The results were disastrous. After only three kings (Saul, David and Solomon) Israel was split in two (Israel and Judah).

WHO BROKE THE COVENANT?

Was God unfaithful to his promises? Did he break any of his covenant promises to Abraham? Or did the people rebel and — in willful defiance — break covenant? Who was responsible for Israel's national trauma? Let's get the answer from the pages of God's word:

"[T]he children of Israel have **forsaken your covenant**, thrown down thine altars, and slain your prophets with the sword...." (*I Kings* 19:10)

"**They kept not the covenant of God**, and refused to walk in his law" (*Psalm* 78:10)

"The earth is also defiled under the inhabitants thereof; because **they** have transgressed the laws, changed the ordinance, **broken the everlasting covenant**" (*Isaiah* 24:5)

"**Nevertheless they were disobedient, and rebelled against you, and cast your law behind their backs**, and slew your prophets which testified against them to turn them to you, and **they wrought great provocations**.

"Therefore you delivered them into the hands of their enemies, who vexed them." When they cried out to God, he — because of his covenant — repeatedly saved them out of the hands of their enemies (*Nehemiah* 9:26,27).

They received repeated warnings, but to no avail: "**And the Lord God of their fathers sent to them by his messengers ... because he had compassion on his people,** and on his dwelling place.

"**But they mocked the messengers of God**, and despised his words, and misused his prophets, **until the wrath of God arose**

ABRAHAMIC COVENANT

against his people, till there was no remedy" (*II Chronicles* 36:15-16).

Pay particular attention to the phrase, "**till there was no remedy**." The physical seed of Abraham had been given every opportunity to repent and change — but didn't. There was no point in continuing; everything that had to be proved had already been established.

It is abundantly clear that God — in his total faithfulness — kept covenant with them (*Nehemiah* 9:28-32). It was clearly the people who rebelled and broke the covenant; as a result, they suffered the consequences. Later, because of their unfaithfulness they lost the land to their enemies (*Nehemiah* 9:37).

Israel went into captivity in 718 B.C.; Judah followed in 604 B.C. The latter became known as the Babylonian Captivity. Jerusalem was destroyed in 587 B.C.

Under the leadership of Ezra and Nehemiah, a faithful remnant of Judah returned to Jerusalem thus enabling Jesus to be born almost five hundred years later in nearby Bethlehem.

CHAPTER 13

THE ABRAHAMIC COVENANT TODAY

Under the New Covenant is physical Israel "God's Chosen People"? Or is there another group of people — individuals with the faith of Abraham — who, by the sovereign grace of God, have now been chosen and are being used by Almighty God? It's vital that we understand the truth.

The Jews of Jesus' day were very proud of their ancestry; as their *Babylonian Talmud* clearly shows, in their pride and smug self-righteousness they considered themselves vastly superior to the common rabble (goyim, or "human cattle") around them in the world. But what did Jesus **("the way, the truth, and the life," John 14:6)** say when he came face-to-face with their leaders?

"But when he saw many of the Pharisees and Sadducees come to his baptism, he said unto them, **O generation of vipers**, who has warned you to flee from the wrath to come?

"Bring forth therefore fruits meet for repentance;

"And **think not** to say **within yourselves**, We have Abraham to our father: **for I say unto you, that God is able of these stones to raise up children unto Abraham.**

"But now also the ax is laid unto the root of the trees; wherefore **every** tree which bringeth **not** forth good fruit **is hewn down and cast into the fire....**" (*Matthew* 7-10). In the first century — and as part of God's sovereign plan — physical Israel was about to be chopped down to make way for another Israel, spiritual Israel — **"the Israel of God"** (*Galatians* 6:16).

Racial "chosenness" was now a thing of the past. Any "chosenness" that may have been enjoyed by physical Israel under the Old Covenant ended with the prophesied birth of Jesus. *And with the death, resurrection, and ascension of Jesus Christ it was no longer a matter of race, but rather one of grace.*

WHO ARE "ABRAHAM'S SEED"?

Notice carefully as Jesus lays the truth on the line in no uncertain terms: "I know that you are Abraham's *seed*; **but** you seek to kill me, *because my word hath no place in you.*

"I speak that which I have seen with **my** father, and **you** do that which you have seen with **your** father.

"They answered and said unto him, Abraham is our father. Jesus said unto them, **If** you were Abraham's *children*, you would **do** the works of Abraham. **[Notice the line that Jesus draws between "Abraham's seed" and "Abraham's children." In this context the two are on opposite sides. One is physical, the other spiritual]**.

"But now you seek to kill me, a man that has told you the truth, which I have heard of God; this did not Abraham.

"*You do the deeds of your father.* Then said they unto him, We be not born of fornication [The *Talmud* teaches that Mary was a whore, and that Jesus was the illegitimate son of a Roman soldier]; we have one father, even God.

"Jesus said unto them, **if** God were your father, **you would love me**; for I proceeded forth and came from God; neither came I of myself, but he sent me.

"**Why do you not understand** my speech? even **because you cannot hear my word**.

"**You are of your father, the devil, and the lusts of your father you will do.** *He was a murderer from the beginning, and abode not in the truth, because there is no truth in him. When he speaks a lie, he speakes of his own, for he is a liar and the father of it.*

"Which of you convinces me of sin? And if I say the truth, why do you not believe me?

"He that is of God hears my voice: you therefore hear them not, because you are not of God" (*John* 8:37-47).

What an explosive statement! These Jews were **not** true children of God. As Jesus clearly stated, they were children of their spiritual father, Satan the Devil. They didn't have "ears to hear" the truth (*Matthew* 4:19).

In this passage and elsewhere, Jesus was speaking, (1) About the physical seed of Abraham, and, (2) The spiritual "children" of Abraham. He was speaking of two entirely different types of person. Let's check that out further.

ABOUT WHOM WAS JESUS SPEAKING?

"Jesus saw Nathaniel coming to him, and said of him, **Behold an Israelite indeed, in whom there is no guile**" (*John* 1:47). The word "indeed" means "truly, indeed, of a surety" (*Strong's Exhaustive Concordance*, reference #230).

Nathaniel was a *true*, spiritual Israelite. As a new breed of "spiritual" Israelite, he was the exact opposite of Jacob whose name had been changed to Israel (*Genesis 32:28*). Jesus is speaking of those who, through the power of God, are "in" him. They are a "new creation: old things are passed away; behold, all things are become new" (*II Corinthians* 5:17). They are the ones whom God has called to enter his kingdom.

Unknown to those around him Zacchaeus was another such "son of Abraham." The Bible tells us that Zacchaeus was "chief among the publicans" [publican: "a tax farmer, i.e. collector of public revenue" (*Strong's Exhaustive Concordance*, reference # 5057)].

As a "tax farmer," Zacchaeus was authorized by the Roman authorities to collect taxes from his fellow Jews. Everything he collected over and above what the Romans demanded was his to keep and use as he wished. As a result Zacchaeus became "rich."

As might be expected, tax farmers were not viewed in a very favorable light by the Jewish society of that day. In fact, they were considered scum; they were placed in the same category as "sinners" and harlots (*Matthew* 9:10,11; 11:19; 21:31, and *Luke* 5:30). In the eyes of the religious leaders Zacchaeus was "lost."

But something happened to Zacchaeus. During the days of Jesus' ministry something began to stir within his heart and mind; changes were taking place. *Luke* chapter 19 records that when Jesus entered and passed through Jericho, Zacchaeus "sought to see Jesus who he was; and could not for the press, because he was small in stature." Running ahead of Jesus and the throng that surrounded him, Zacchaeus climbed up a sycamore tree to get a better view. Seeing him there, Jesus said to him: "Zacchaeus, make haste, and come down; for today I must abide at your house.

"And he made haste, and came down, and received him joyfully."

Now, notice the reaction of the crowd: "[T]hey all murmured, saying, That he is gone to be guest with a man that is a sinner."

Zacchaeus made no excuses; he immediately acknowledged all his sins — his double dealings, his thievery, and his chicanery as a "tax farmer." Turning around and going the other way, he repented deeply of his past activities.

Upon his acknowledgment of his sin and declaration of repentance, "Jesus said unto him [Zacchaeus], This day has salvation come to this house, forasmuch as he is a son of Abraham.

"For the Son of man is come to seek and to save that which was lost" (*Luke* 19:9,10).

By faith in Christ Zacchaeus was now "a son of Abraham." He had been "born again." He was a "new creation: old things [were] passed away; behold, all things [were] become new" (*II Corinthians* 5:17).

THE KINGDOM OF GOD

At the start of his earthly ministry, "Jesus ... came preaching the gospel of God" (*Mark* 1:14). The phrase "kingdom of God" (69 times) or "kingdom of heaven" (32 times) are used interchangeably throughout the gospels and epistles.

When Jesus sent his disciples out, they carried the same message: "And as you go, preach, saying, The kingdom of heaven is at hand" (*Matthew* 10:7).

When questioned by **his disciples** as to why he spoke in parables, Jesus explained: "Because it is **given** unto **you** to know the mysteries of the kingdom of heaven, **but** to them [the multitude, or masses, see vs. 1-3] it is **not** given" (*Matthew* 13:11). In the gospel according to Mark, Jesus elaborates: "Unto you it is **given** to **know** the mystery of the kingdom of God: **but to them that are without**, all these things are done in parables" (*Mark* 4:11)

Jesus further explained: "I speak to them in parables: **because** they seeing see not; and hearing they hear not, neither do they understand.

"And in them is fulfilled the prophecy of Isaiah which said, By hearing you shall hear, and **shall not** understand; and seeing you shall see, and **shall not** perceive.

"For this people's heart is waxed gross, and their ears are dull of hearing, and their eyes they have closed; lest at any time they *should* see with their eyes, **and** hear with their ears, **and** should understand with their heart, **and should be converted, and I should heal them**.

"But blessed be **your** eyes for **they** see: and **your** ears, for **they** hear.

"For verily I say unto **you**, That **many** prophets and righteous men have desired to see those things that **you** see, and have **not** seen them; and to hear those things that **you** hear, and have **not** heard them" (*Matthew* 13:15-17).

In other words, those who are called by Jesus are **given** special "eyes" and "ears." They — and they alone — have, by God's sovereign grace, been **given** the ability to see, hear, and understand spiritual reality. As Jesus said, "**You** have **not** chosen me, but **I** have chosen you" (*John* 15:16). And again, "**My sheep hear my voice**, and **I know them**, and **they** follow me" *(John* 10:27).

THE SPIRITUALLY DEAD

Elsewhere, Jesus made another statement that probably enrages many: "Let the dead bury the dead: but go you and preach the kingdom of God" (*Luke* 9:60).

Don't spend your time attempting to "convert" those who are spiritually dead — those who haven't been **given** the spiritual "eyes" and "ears" by the Lord Jesus Christ that would enable them to see, hear, and understand spiritual realities. Let them take care of their own duties and responsibilities.

LIKE A GRAIN OF MUSTARD SEED

In Luke's gospel, Jesus asks — and answers — another vital question: "Unto what is the kingdom of heaven like? and whereunto shall I resemble it?

"It is **like** a grain of mustard seed, which a man took, and cast into his garden; and it grew, and waxed a great tree; and the fowls of the air lodged in the branches of it.

"And again he said, Whereunto shall I liken the Kingdom of God?

"It is **like** leaven, which a woman took and **hid** in three measures of meal, till the whole was leavened" (*Luke* 13:18-21).

Jesus is here illustrating a spiritual truth with a physical analogy. When Jesus calls individuals into his kingdom, he — unknown to them — miraculously drops spiritual insights, knowledge, and understanding into their spiritual "ears" which up to that time had lain dormant. He begins to place spiritual truths before their spiritual "eyes" which had hitherto been blinded.

Like a grain of mustard seed — the tiniest of all seeds — this may initially go virtually unnoticed by the recipients. Then, as the spiritual seed slowly starts to grow, mature, and develop, the individuals gradually realize that their thinking, their outlook on life, their worldview have begun — without any conscious effort on their part — to change in some extraordinary manner. Beliefs, values, and attitudes that were earlier held in high esteem are suddenly seen to be threadbare and meaningless. New values, insights, understanding, and perceptions slowly begin to form in their hearts and minds; slowly but surely, these take over and direct their lives. They are now a "new creation: old things are passed away; behold, all things are become new" (*II Corinthians* 5:17).

"For by grace are you saved through faith; **and that not of yourselves: it is the gift of God**" (*Ephesians* 2:8). The process of spiritual regeneration is totally supernatural.

WHO ARE THE TRUE ISRAELITES?

"Then said he unto the multitude that came forth to be baptized of him, O generation of vipers, who hath warned you to flee from the wrath to come.

"Bring forth therefore fruits worthy of repentance, and begin **not** to say within yourselves, We have Abraham to our father: for I say unto you, **That God is able of these stones to raise up children unto Abraham**" (*Luke* 1:7-8).

SALVATION IS BY GRACE, NOT RACE
"**Not as though the word of God hath taken none effect**, For they are **not** all Israel [Spiritual], which are of Israel [Physical].

"**Neither, because they are of the seed** of Abraham, are they all children, **but in Isaac shall your seed be called.**

"That is, They which are of the children of the flesh, these are **not** the children of God: **but the children of the promise are counted for the seed.**

"**For this is the word of promise**, At this time will I come and Sarah **shall** have a son" (**Romans** 9:6-8).

CHILDREN OF THE PROMISE? WHAT GOD DOES WHEN IT IS IMPOSSIBLE FOR MAN TO DO ANYTHING
"Now I say that **Jesus Christ** was a minister of the circumcision for the truth of God, *to confirm the promises made unto the fathers*" (*Romans* 15:8).

"For **all the promises of God** in him are **yea**, and **in him amen**, unto the glory of God for us" (**II Corinthians** 1:20). Jesus Christ is "the Alpha and the Omega, the beginning and ending" of all things (*Revelation* 1:8).

ALL THE PROPHECIES OF GOD ARE SUMMED UP BY AND CONFIRMED IN CHRIST
"That **the blessings of Abraham** might come to the gentiles through Jesus Christ; **that we might receive the promise of the Spirit through faith.**

"Brethren, I speak after the manner of men; Though it be but a man's covenant, yet if it be confirmed, no man disannuleth, or addeth thereto.

"Now to Abraham and his **seed** were the promises made. **He saith NOT, and to seeds [plural] as of many; but as of ONE, And to your seed, which is Christ**" (*Galatians* 3:14-16).

"Even as Abraham believed God, and it was accounted to him for righteousness.

"Know you [gentiles] therefore that **they which are of faith, the same are the children of Abraham.**

"And the scripture, **foreseeing** that God would justify the **heathen** through faith, **preached before the gospel unto Abraham**, saying, **In you shall all nations be blessed**"

"So then they which be of faith are blessed with faithful Abraham" (*Romans* 9:7-9).

"For **you** are **all children of God by faith in Christ Jesus**.

"For **as many of you as** have been baptized into Christ **have put on Christ**.

"There is **neither Jew nor Greek**, there is neither bond nor free, there is neither male nor female; **for you are all one in Christ Jesus**.

"And **if** you be Christ's, **then are you Abraham's seed and heirs according to the promises** (*Galatians* 3:26-29).

This glorious fact is still further emphasized by the Apostle Paul: "For they are **not** all [spiritual] Israel [i.e., Abraham's seed, and heirs according to the promises] which are of [physical] Israel.

"**Neither** because they **are** the (physical) seed of Abraham, are they all children: but, In Isaac shall your seed be called.

"That is, They which are **the children of the flesh**, these are **not** the children of God; but **the children of the promise** (what God does when it is impossible for man to do anything) **are** counted for the seed" (*Romans* 9:6-8). These are the people who are known in scripture as "the Israel of God" (*Galatians* 6:16). These are the people ("my people Israel," *Matthew* 1:6) over whom Jesus — the Governor — rules.

Chapter 14

BIBLICAL CHRISTIANITY

> "This know also, that in the last days perilous times shall come.
> "For men shall be lovers of their own selves, covetous, boasters, proud, blasphemers, disobedient to parents, unthankful, unholy,
> "Without natural affection, trucebreakers, false accusers, incontinent [licentious], fierce, despisers of those that are good,
> "Traitors, heady, highminded, lovers of pleasures more than lovers of God,
> "Having a form of godliness, but denying the power thereof: from such turn away....
> "Ever learning but never able to come to a knowledge of the truth" (*II Timothy* 3:1-5,7).

Could anything more perfectly describe our world in the waning days of the twentieth century? Hardly! Ours is the "ME" generation — a generation dedicated to the relentless pursuit of every vice that our carnal minds can conceive; jealousy, vanity, lust, and greed are the guiding principles which influence the world in which we live.

The old fashioned virtues of honesty, sincerity, integrity, reliability, truthfulness, faithfulness — all based on absolute values — are ridiculed and held in contempt. A philosophical attitude of, "I'll get mine while the getting's good, and let the next guy be damned" appears to be the motivating force in all too many lives.

Clearly, the world is in a fallen state and manifesting the "works of the flesh" as enumerated in *Galatians* 5:19-21: "Adultery, fornication, uncleanness, lasciviousness, idolatry, witchcraft, hatred, variance, emulations, wrath, strife, seditions, heresies, envyings, murders, drunkenness, revellings, and such like...."

As phrased by the Apostle Paul in another scripture (*Ephesians* 2:1), the world is "dead in [its] trespasses and sins." And, as yet another verse states, "[A]ll that is in the world, the lust of the flesh, and the lust of the eyes, and the pride of life, is not of the Father, but is of the world" (*I John* 2:16). *In their natural condition the people of the world are "strangers from the covenants of promise, having no hope, and without God in the world*" (*Ephesians* 2:12).

TWO BASIC TRUTHS

Before we can hold out any hope of changing the situation, we must first acknowledge two very basic truths: (1) Human nature is a constant — it dominates and controls every human being, and (2) Without divine intervention it is impossible to truly change.

These facts are, of course, angrily denied by the vast, overwhelming majority. To them, it is totally repugnant to even suggest they might be "dead in their sins," and thus have "no hope." The truth is so psychologically disruptive and ego-shattering that it must be denied and rejected from every point of the compass. The carnal, fleshly mind with which we are all born — and which the Bible clearly states is "enmity against God" and "not subject to the law of God, neither indeed can be" (*Romans* 8:7) — automatically produces a dazzling array of arguments and excuses which deny reality. It will insist that up is down, that right is wrong, that good is bad, that black is white, and that man is perfectly capable of running his own show without any interference from God (if, perchance, he might possibly exist). Talk about total denial! "[T]his is the condemnation, that light is come into the world, and men loved darkness rather than light because their deeds were evil.

"For everyone that does evil hates the light, neither comes to the light, lest his deeds should be reproved" (*John* 1:19,20).

REPROBATE MIND

Particularly in today's society, such denial is to be expected. This is the only generation in American history that has completely turned its back on the knowledge of God and reverence for His Word: "And even as they did not like to retain God in their knowledge [educational system], God gave them over to a **reprobate** mind" (*Romans* 1:28).

What is a reprobate mind? It is one that "is abandoned to sin; lost to virtue or grace.... Abandoned to error, or in apostasy" (Webster's *Dictionary of the English Language*, 1828).

And what is the result of the insanity produced by reprobate minds? The society becomes "filled with all unrighteousness, fornication, wickedness, covetousness, maliciousness; full of envy, murder, debate, deceit, malignity; whisperers."

It becomes filled with, "Backbiters, haters of God, despiteful, proud, boasters, inventors of evil things, disobedient to parents;

"Without understanding, covenantbreakers, without natural affection, implacable [unrelenting], unmerciful;

"Who knowing the judgment of God, that they which commit such things are worthy of death, not only do the same, but have pleasure in them that do them" (*Romans* 1:29-32).

Yet another devastating indictment of today's society, written 2000 years ago!

Throughout the Bible — in both the Old and New Testaments — these basic facts are repeatedly confirmed and underlined: "The heart of man is deceitful above all things, and desperately wicked; who can know it?" (*Jeremiah* 17:9). Man is naturally at "enmity with God...." (*Romans* 8:7). Now, pay particular attention to the last part of this verse. It is one of the most important statements in the Bible relating to man's natural condition. **Man "is not subject to the law of God, neither indeed can be."** Of, by, and through his own efforts — and regardless of how hard he may try — man cannot become subject to God's law. As we learned earlier, he is spiritually "dead in trespasses and sins" (*Ephesians* 2:1). All such futile efforts are, in fact, forms of artificial respiration; they lead to still further frustration, mental anguish, and burnout.

THE WAY TO GOD?

In chapter 10 we saw the futility of Churchianity and Religion, both of which have turned their backs on God's word and developed their own devious ways of allegedly "coming to God." No amount of emotional fervor, playacting, ritual, or spiritual mumbo-jumbo can cover up the fact that they have failed miserably in their puny efforts to fill people's deepest spiritual and psychological needs. No amount of artificial respiration or emotional hype can explain away or cover up the spiritual bankruptcy that has been their legacy. By their fruit shall you know them!

Politics is even worse. During this twentieth century, man, in his deep-seated rebellion against God — and in his unwillingness to face the truth about himself — has set about establishing himself into the collective form of man, the state, and as god.

Before the time of Christ such practices and claims were commonplace among the leaders of the "great" world empires — Egypt, Assyria, Babylon, Medo-Persia, Greece, and Rome. What we are witnessing, particularly during the latter half of the twentieth century is the reemergence of this phenomenon on the world scene for the first time in 2,000 years. It is just another attempt to replace the rule of God with the rule of collective man, the rule of the state.

The true significance of this will be explained in the final chapter.

As we saw in a previous chapter, the seeds of this phenomenon were sown in 1776 with the creation by Adam Weishaupt of the Illuminati (the Order of the Enlightened Ones). In the nineteenth century these seeds gradually took root; in this century they sprang up and manifested themselves in various forms: Humanism, Socialism, Fabianism, Communism, Fascism, Liberalism, etc.

All have been tried extensively; all have failed abysmally!

Their humanistic renunciation of God, their denial of absolute truths and the existence of sin, their rejection of knowledge about the true nature of man, and their promotion of "situation ethics," leads to serious problems. For instance, sexual perversion is classified as an "alternative lifestyle" and shoplifting as "alternative shopping." They believe that people are the product of their environment, and that man, through social engineering, behavior modification, and the control and manipulation of society, can be his own messiah. These Utopian pipe dreams based on man's own incredible ego, wishful thinking, and false sense of self worth, have all abysmally failed.

In this fantasy world of liberal lunacy "there is no objectivity or truth. Everything is relative. Nothing is better or truer than anything else. Knowledge is politically constructed, an extension of power" (*U.S. New and World Report*, August 7, 1995).

The legacy of this humanistic dementia (man's belief in the Satanic lie that he can be "as god" [*Genesis* 3:5]) is everywhere evident: bigger and ever more intrusive and dictatorial government, the negating of personal responsibility, less and less personal freedom, higher and higher taxes, ever-increasing lawlessness — and societies worldwide that are sinking ever-deeper into manmade depravity. The Satan-inspired ideologies that promised gullible mankind a Utopian dreamworld have in fact created conditions that are fast degenerating into a hellish nightmare euphemistically called the New World Order. The NWO will be a global concentration camp controlled by the Illuminated ones: a government of the elite, by the elite, and for the elite.

Lost man — under the influence of his reprobate mind — is in total denial of reality. In this condition, the response of collective man will continue to be: "Just give us one more chance; we still have a few problems that need to be sorted out, but we can make it. We don't need any help. We can do it all ourselves."

Mankind — like its creations, Churchianity and Religion — is in desperate need of a true Savior, but will deny and fight that reality till its dying breath.

WHERE DO WE GO FROM HERE?

If we acknowledge the fact that churchianity, religion, and the various manmade political schemes allegedly designed for the betterment of mankind have failed miserably to achieve their alleged objectives, it would be very easy for us to throw our hands up in the air, and — in a state of utter despair — abandon all hope of ever finding anything purposeful in life. Thus marinating in despair, it would be equally easy for us to embrace the fatalistic outlook of, "Posterity be damned! Let's eat, drink, and be merry for tomorrow we die."

Prevailing conditions in the United States strongly suggest that most Americans have adopted such an outlook. As a result, their's is a life of frustration and anguish — and one into which they attempt to cram as many forms and variations of artificial respiration as is humanly possible. But the end result, the ever-present bottom line is always the same: DEEP DESPAIR.

The message of Religion is one of man frantically trying to put together the broken pieces of his life and, then, desperately reaching up to some nebulous, undefined Deity, pleading for mercy, forgiveness, and possibly salvation. It is one of man despairingly attempting to placate a wrathful God with all the religiously-appropriate whimpering and whining they can muster.

Although the Bible, God, Jesus Christ, and the Holy Spirit are mentioned intermittently, you will notice that man is always the central figure in this type of scenario. Man initiates the action, and — if he tries hard enough — his endeavors eventually lead to his acceptance by God; in other words, he does most of the work! In theological terminology, this doctrine is known as "free will" or Arminianism.

The religious life is perceived to be one of relentless struggle, as the individuals involved attempt to appease the anger of God and get on his right side. Though it will be denied by most, in its many forms, guises, and disguises, the bottom line is the same: **attempted salvation by works!**

That is **not** the gospel (Good News) of Jesus Christ. It is, in fact, very bad news; it promotes the Satanic lie that man can "be as god" and thus instrumental in saving himself (*Genesis* 3:5). It is, in truth, the manifestation of "another gospel" and "another Jesus" as warned against by the Apostle Paul.

SOVEREIGN GRACE

Now at last we come to Biblical Christianity — and the true gospel (the truly good news) as expounded in the pages of God's Word.

Biblical Christianity **is not** the story of carnal man frantically **reaching up** to God and asking for some help in bettering himself.

Biblical Christianity **is** the story of the Almighty, Sovereign Creator God **reaching down** from his Throne of Grace to pick totally helpless, spiritually dead, mentally diseased reprobates up out of the Satanically-controlled seething cesspool of iniquity we know as today's society on planet earth. In theological terms, it's called Sovereign Grace, i.e. it's the work of the Sovereign God acting alone as Ruler of heaven and earth; no other factors are involved. Grace is the free unmerited love and favor of God, the spring and source of all the benefits man receives from him.

"And if by grace, then it is no more of works" (*Romans* 11:6).

This is solely and exclusively God's doing. Man has no say in the matter. One's "righteousness" or "unrighteousness" has nothing to do with being saved by grace: "By grace are you saved through faith; and that **not** of yourselves: it is the **gift** of God.

"**Not** of works, **lest** any man should boast" (*Ephesians* 2:8,9).

No recipient of God's grace can say, "God obviously called me because I was so good, so righteous, and so dedicated to his truth that I deserved it." In the same vein, God doesn't say to anyone, "After all the great work you've done on my behalf, the least I can do for you is...."

"**For you see your calling brethren**, how not many wise men after the flesh, not many mighty, not many noble are called.

"But God has chosen the foolish things of the world to confound the wise; and God has chosen the weak things of the world to confound the things that are mighty;

"And base things, and things which are despised, has God chosen, yes, and things that are not, to bring to nought things that are.

"**That no flesh should glory in his presence**" (*I Corinthians* 1:26-29).

God never has to say "Ooops!" after he calls someone. He never makes a mistake, "For the gifts and calling of God are without repentance" (*Romans* 11:29)

IN THE LAMB'S BOOK OF LIFE

The book of Romans (especially chapters 8-11) is a treasure chest of knowledge and understanding on Sovereign Grace.

Scripture clearly reveals that those to be called were elected when they were "**not** yet born, **neither** having done **any** good **or** evil, that the purpose of God through election might stand, **not of works, but of him that calls**" (*Romans* 9:11). Could anything be clearer? Their names were in the Lamb's book of life "from the foundation of the world" (*Revelation* 13:8; 17:8).

It is after their calling by God — after they have begun to have their spiritual "eyes" and "ears" opened by the Sovereign Grace of God that they are called upon to, "Repent and be baptized ... in the name of [or by the authority of] Jesus Christ for the remission of sins." They then "receive the gift of the Holy Spirit" (*Acts* 2:38).

WHAT IS REPENTANCE?

What is Repentance? Real repentanc is sorrow or deep contrition for sin, as an offense and dishonor to God, a violation of his holy law, and the basest ingratitude towards a Being of infinite benevolence.

True repentance is, in fact, an open and unreserved acknowledgment of, and turning away from, what you really **are** as revealed by God's word. It is an acknowledgment of, deep sorrow over, and immediate turning away from the fact that you were deceived into believing the Satanic lie that you could be "as god." It is the wholehearted recognition of the fact that, but for the priceless grace of God, you would still be "dead in your trespasses and sins ... and without hope in the world."

You repent of what you **are**, because that is the source of all your actions. King David declared the truth when he said to God: "Against you, you only, have I sinned, and done this evil in your sight" (*Psalm* 51:4). God is a "jealous God." He doesn't like competition.

Jesus said in another place, "I came not to call the 'righteous,' but sinners to repentance" (*Luke* 5:32). In that context, we are assured by God's word that there is "joy ... in heaven over one sinner that repents, more than over ninety nine 'just' persons which [supposedly] need no repentance" (*Luke* 15:7).

Jesus has little interest in those smug, self-righteous individuals who make up the ranks in Churchianity and Religion — whose who believe that their good works will save them. Instead, he targets those who, by the grace of God, are able to see — with their new, God-given spiritual eyes — the depths of their own personal unworthiness and sin. By the grace of God, they are also able to see that their own "righteousness is as filthy rags" (*Isaiah* 64:6), and that — through the atoning blood of the Lord Jesus Christ — though their "sins be as scarlet they shall be as white as snow; though they be red like crimson, they shall be as wool" (*Isaiah* 1:18). They at last begin to see and understand the awesome righteousness, love, and mercy of the Sovereign God — and the astonishing price that Jesus paid on Calvary's cross for their personal redemption.

They also begin to see, again by the grace of God, that he is not interested in some humanly devised form of offering — like that presented by Cain and rejected by God in *Genesis* 4:1-8. Rather, God requires that the brethren of Christ "present [their] bodies a living sacrifice, holy, acceptable unto God" (*Romans* 12:1). Christ wants disciples (those who will sacrificially submit themselves to his discipline), not "sunshine followers" who can't be relied upon.

Again, by their fruits shall you know them!

"SAVED BY HIS LIFE"

But the death of Jesus Christ doesn't save anyone eternally; it "just" redeems them from the penalty of their sins. It "justifies" them **(makes them just as if they had never sinned)**. It pays the price demanded by the Righteous God, but it doesn't save them.

Had Jesus Christ not been raised from the dead on the third day (*I Corinthians* 15:4; *Acts* 10:40; *Matthew* 20:19), any hope of or faith in a future life would have been in vain. They would still be "in their sins" (*I Corinthians* 15:13-18).

It is the resurrection of Jesus Christ which broke the grip that Satan had on them. It was the ascension of the risen Jesus Christ (the perfect sacrificial lamb and the type of the Old Covenant wave offering) into the Holy of Holies in heaven that opened up the way to atonement (**at-one-ment**) between God and man. As the Apostle Paul declared, "we also joy in God through Jesus Christ our Lord, *by whom we have now received the atonement*" (*Romans* 5:11).

THE LAW OF BIOGENESIS

The people of God are redeemed (bought back from sin and reconciled to God) by the shed blood (death) of Jesus Christ. But there has to be more. The law of biogenesis dictates that life (salvation) cannot come through a dead Christ. The law of biogenesis states that life can only come from life — preexisting life of the same kind.

In order to become Savior and thus "save his people from their sins" (*Matthew* 1:21), Jesus Christ had to be raised from the dead. The reader will remember that during his earthly ministry, one of the signs (or proofs) Jesus gave of his Messiahship was the fact that he would rise from the dead on the third day (*John* 2:18-19).

Let scripture nail down these vital points: "**For if, when we were enemies, we were reconciled to God by the death of his Son, much more being reconciled, we shall be saved by his life**" (*Romans* 5:10). Redemption, reconciliation, and atonement come through the death of Jesus Christ; life and salvation come through the resurrection and present spiritual life of Jesus Christ. It is "Christ in you [which is your] hope of glory" (*Colossians* 1:27). It is "Christ who is our life" (*Colossians* 3:4).

The death of Jesus Christ had even greater significance. Through the shedding of his blood was sealed the New Covenant which God had promised to make with his people (*Jeremiah* 31:31-). The wonderful fact that the New Covenant is now in full force and effect is demonstrated by the Apostle Paul: "But **now has he obtained** a more excellent ministry, by how much also he **is** the mediator of **a better covenant which was established upon better promises**....

"In that he says, a better covenant, he has made the first old. Now that which decays and waxes old is ready [in the first century] to vanish away" (*Hebrews* 8:6,13). Of course! As we saw at the conclusion of chapter 9, the Old Covenant (Testament) promises to Abraham were completed in Christ: "If you are Christ's, **then** are you Abraham's seed and heirs according to the promise" (*Galatians* 3:29). More on this new covenant later.

"HE LED CAPTIVITY CAPTIVE"

Something else of tremendous importance resulted from the death, resurrection and ascension of Jesus Christ: "When he ascended up on high, he led captivity captive and gave gifts unto men" (*Ephesians* 4:8).

In this scripture — in order to drive home to the Christians of the first century the power and significance of Christ's victory over Satan — the Apostle Paul draws an analogy with a victorious Roman general who has won a glorious victory over the enemies of his people. That enemy used to hold a remnant of his subjects in bondage, but now they have been miraculously freed.

As conqueror through his death, resurrection, and ascension — and as a result of having been given "all power ... in heaven and in earth" (*Matthew* 28:18) — Christ is now parading his defeated foe (Satan) before his redeemed elect to celebrate his victory and demonstrate to them the impotence of their former slavemaster. Not only that but, in addition, Christ gives his people special, invaluable gifts.

God's elect who were Satan's slaves (and "dead in their trespasses and sins" [*Ephesians* 2:1]), have been freed by the grace of God, and given the gift of the Holy Spirit, participation in the New Covenant, and all the attendant spiritual gifts and blessings.

"God has not given us the spirit of fear; but of power, and of love, and of a sound mind" (*II Timothy* 1:7). By the process of logical deduction and elimination, we can see that only those who have and are led by the Holy Spirit have a truly "sound mind."

No Holy Spirit, no truly sound mind!

As Jesus said, "By their fruits shall you know them: "[T]he **fruit** of the Spirit **is** love, joy, peace, longsuffering, gentleness, goodness, faith, meekness, temperance; against such there is no law" (*Galatians* 5:22-23). Those who are not led by the Holy Spirit produce, instead, the **works** of the flesh (*Galatians* 5:19-21).

"By grace are you saved through faith; and that not of yourselves: *it is the gift of God.*

"**Not** of works, **lest** any man should boast" (*Ephesians* 2:8,9).

Notice in *Galatians* chapter five that spiritual fruit comes through the Holy Spirit; works come from the flesh — man's owns efforts.

AMAZING GRACE

How is God's grace and mercy best expressed? Perhaps in the life, conversion, and words of John Newton.

John Newton (1725-1807) was a wonderful example of God's amazing grace. In the 1740s, after working for six years on a ship of which his father was master, Newton was forced to serve on board a man-of-war, where he was made mid-shipman. For an attempt to escape he was publicly flogged and degraded. After this experience he joined another vessel bound for Africa; there, he served under a slave dealer. In 1747 he returned to the sea, and for a time became captain of a slave ship; he gave up his seafaring life in 1755.

Newton — previously well-known for his unbelief and blasphemy — underwent a dramatic conversion during a storm at sea in 1748. Later, as a friend of George Whitefield and John Wesley, and after studying Greek and Hebrew, he went on to have a very influential ministry (*Encyclopedia Britannica*, 1971).

Since his death in London in 1807, millions of people have been inspired and uplifted by his most famous hymns, *Amazing Grace*, *Glorious Things of Thee are Spoken*, and *How Sweet the Name of Jesus Sounds*.

BIBLICAL CHRISTIANITY

In the first hymn, Newton — in just 99 words — verbalizes what every one who has had a true conversion experience would express if they only had the ability to condense and focus their personal thoughts on, and reactions to, God's Amazing Grace.

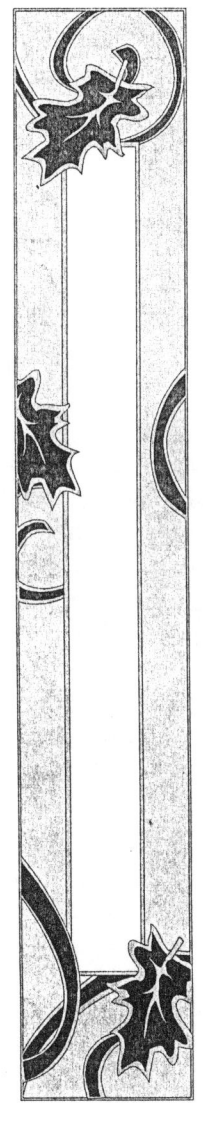

> Amazing grace! how sweet the sound,
> That saved a wretch like me!
> I once was lost, but now am found,
> Was blind, but now I see
>
> 'Twas grace that taught my heart to fear,
> And grace my fears relieved;
> How precious did that grace appear
> The hour I first believed!
>
> Thro' many dangers, toils, and snares,
> I have already come;
> 'Tis grace that bro't me safe thus far,
> And Grace will lead me home.
>
> When we've been there
> ten thousand years,
> Bright shining as the sun,
> We've no less days to sing God's praise
> Than when we first begun.

CHAPTER 15

THE NEW TESTAMENT CHURCH

Throughout the books of the Old Testament — from *Genesis* to *Malachi* — mankind is directed, often in types or shadows, to look forward to the coming of the Messiah who would redeem mankind. There are dozens of prophecies in the Old Testament which were fulfilled in the birth, life, ministry, death, resurrection, and ascension of Jesus Christ. A few such scriptures are: *Genesis* 3:15; 12:3; 49:10; *Deuteronomy* 15:13; *Psalm* 2:2; *Isaiah* 9:6,7; 11:1,2; *Daniel* 2:34,44; 9:25; *Zechariah* 3:8; 6:12; 9:9; *Malachi* 3:1.

In the New Testament the emphasis is totally on Jesus Christ. He is the one who saves **his** people **from** their sins (*Matthew* 1:21; *John* 4:25,26). He has been given all power in heaven and in earth (*Matthew* 28:18); He is the light of the world (*John* 8:12); He is the bread of life (*John* 6:48). Jesus is the door through whom people must enter into the kingdom of God; He is the way, the truth, and the life (*John* 14:6). He is our life (*Colossians* 2:4). Christ in us is the hope of glory (*Colossians* 1:27).

Jesus Christ is the author of salvation to all who obey him (*Hebrews* 5:9); he is the author and finisher of our faith (*Hebrews* 12:2). The stone [Jesus Christ, *Ephesians* 2:20] which was set at nought by the builders **is** become the head of the corner on which God's church is built.

"Neither is there salvation in any other name: **for** there is none other name under heaven given among men, whereby we must be saved" (*Acts* 4:11,12). He is the same yesterday, today, and forever more (*Hebrews* 13:8).

Jesus Christ is the faithful witness (*Revelation* 1:5); he is the Alpha and Omega, the beginning and the ending (*Revelation* 1:8,11).

If he is all of those things — **and he is** — what else is there?

Truly, he is "worthy ... to receive glory and honor and power for [he] has created all things, and for [his] pleasure they are were created" (*Revelation* 4:11).

THE BOOK OF REVELATION

The servants or saints to whom the book of Revelation was written (1:1) were simple, unsophisticated, first-century Christian people; they were everyday folks. If anything, they were below average in both natural ability and wealth: "For you see your calling brethren, how that not many wise men after the flesh, not many mighty, not many noble, are called.

"But God has chosen the foolish things of the world to confound the wise; and God has chosen the weak things of the world to confound the things which are [considered by most to be] mighty.

"And base things of the world, and things which are despised [by most people], has God chosen, yes, and things which are not, to bring to nought things that are [considered to be great].

"That no flesh should glory in his presence" (*I Corinthians* 1:29-29).

"Listen, my beloved brethren, Has not God chosen the poor of this world rich in faith, and heirs of the kingdom which he had promised to them that love him" (*James* 2:5).

They had been called out of their various sin-laden societies and cultures to repentance toward God and faith in Jesus Christ. They had been "buried with him by baptism into death; that like as Christ was raised up from the dead by the glory of the Father, even so [they] should walk in newness of life" (*Romans* 6:4). They had also been given the gift of the Holy Spirit — the spirit "of power, and of love, and of a sound mind" (*I Timothy* 1:7).

THEY NEEDED ENCOURAGEMENT

They had been called, not for their several abilities but by the Sovereign grace of Almighty God. As "babes in Christ" (*I Corinthians* 3:1) they needed guidance and encouragement. As they grew in grace and in the knowledge of their Lord and Savior Jesus Christ (*II Peter* 3:18), they needed to be uplifted in the faith and "strengthened with the might of [God's] spirit in the inner man; That Christ [might] dwell in [their] hearts by faith; [that they might be] rooted and grounded in love" (*Ephesians* 3:16,17).

Notice, briefly, how the book of *Revelation* concludes: "The grace of our Lord Jesus Christ be with **you all**. Amen" (22:21). Who are "you all"? They are the same "servants" of God mentioned in chapter 1:1. This whole book is targeted **exclusively** at them — nobody else. They — and they alone — are able to understand it.

They all "get the message" — and Jesus Christ gets all the glory. Praise God!

NUMEROUS INTERPRETATIONS

Regrettably for the people of God, the mid-to-late twentieth century has witnessed the emergence of numerous grotesquely fantastic interpretations of the book of *Revelation*. Dozens of books and hundreds of articles have been written about it; as a result, bewilderment reigns in the religious community.

Unfortunately, many of God's people (his servants) have been caught up in the confusion and are thus missing out on the many blessings promised those who read and understand the book (*Revelation* 1:3; 16:15; 19:9; 22:7). It is essential to bear in mind at all times the identity of those to whom this book is directed: God's servants — those whom he has called by his sovereign grace. Everyone else is reading other people's mail, and their interpretations of the book come from their own fleshly, vain imaginations — not from God!

All things must be done decently and in order (*I Corinthians* 14:40). In reading the book of *Revelation*, one must remember that "no prophecy of the scripture is of any private interpretation" (*II Peter* 1:20). As is true with all scripture, *Revelation* is "not in the words which man's wisdom teaches, but which the Holy Ghost [Spirit] teacheth; comparing spiritual things with spiritual" (*I Corinthians* 2:13).

Anyone who ignores this truth is left wallowing in confusion.

Those who are truly God's people have the divine assurance that "The spirit of truth ... will guide [them] into all truth" (*John* 16:13). As a result "they shall know the truth, and the truth shall make [them] free" (*John* 8:32).

THE TESTIMONY OF JESUS CHRIST

The book of *Revelation* was written by the Apostle John on the Isle of Patmos about 94 A.D. John bore faithful record of both the word of God and the testimony of Jesus Christ (v.2). First, notice that this book is the Revelation **of** Jesus Christ, which God **gave** to him **to show unto his servants** things which must shortly come to pass. Note that God sent and **signified** the message by his angel unto his servant John (1:1). In other words, it was a private message from God, through Christ, to his saints, the church — the body of Christ (*Ephesians* 5:23). In addition, it was given in signs and symbols (a sign is a physical symbol for a spiritual reality).

It should go without saying that the message was designed to **reveal** the love and will of God **to** his servants. It was **not** designed to conceal God's will and thus confuse his people. However, as the church at that time was under tremendous persecution — with its members living in constant fear for their lives — the book may have been at least partly written to conceal from the Roman authorities the true makeup of the church; had they known the truth, the Romans would no doubt have made it even harder on the church.

[It is important that we note in passing that after Jesus had risen from the dead he appeared **only** to those people whom he had called and selected. He never appeared to any of the religious or political leaders].

As the result of having "another king, one Jesus" (*Acts* 17:7), Christians were very unpopular with the authorities. However, in the final analysis, it wasn't individual Christians who were being persecuted — it was Jesus Christ. When Saul of Tarsus ("breathing out threatenings and slaughter against the disciples of the Lord") was on the road to Damascus during his mad rampage against the early church, he was met along the way by the risen Lord. After he had been blinded by a light from heaven, he heard a voice: "Saul, Saul, why do you persecute me? I am Jesus whom you persecute" (*Acts* 9:4,5). This incident quickly led to the conversion of Saul, whose name was then changed to Paul. As a result, one of the most hatefilled enemies of the early church became its most ardent defender and spokesman.

ONE OF ITS DARKEST HOURS

This revelation of the living, reigning Jesus Christ was given by God to his church during one of its darkest hours. As we shall see, it was designed to call the attention of God's servants to many wonderfully encouraging spiritual realities; the body of Christ would thus be encouraged and strengthened in its hour of trial.

CHRIST REIGNS IN THE MIDST OF HIS CHURCH

With that overview clearly in mind, the spiritual reality of the messages contained in the book begins to unfold. To ensure that his people would immediately grasp the significance and purpose of the book, God gives John a vision. John was told to write what he saw in a book and to send it to the seven churches that were in Asia: Ephesus, Smyrna, Pergamos, Thyatira, Sardis, Philadelphia, and Laodicea. In the vision, John "saw seven golden candlesticks; And in the midst of the candlesticks was one like unto the Son of man [Christ, see *Matthew* 8:20, *Mark* 2:10].... He had in his right hand seven stars, and out of his mouth went a sharp two-edged sword: and his countenance was as the sun shines in his strength."

At this sight, John fell down as if dead. Christ then laid his hand on John, saying: "Fear not; I am the first and the last.

"I am he that lives and was dead; and, behold, **I am alive for ever more**, Amen; and have the keys of hell and of death.

"Write the things that you have seen, and the things which are, and the things which shall be hereafter;

"The mystery of the seven stars which you saw in my right hand, and the seven golden candlesticks. The seven stars **are** the angels of the seven churches; and the seven candlesticks which you saw **are** the seven churches" (*Revelation* 1:10-20).

This sets the scene for the whole book. Here we see the risen, victorious — "alive for evermore" — Jesus Christ working invisibly in the midst of his people at the end of the first century — more than sixty years after his death, resurrection, and ascension. The number seven (a complete number) denotes the complete company of God's people — his church — in Asia. Each of the seven churches had a

THE NEW TESTAMENT CHURCH

guardian angel. Scripture shows that God's people are constantly guarded and protected by angels (see, *Acts* 12:8; 29:23; *Hebrews* 13:2).

The activities, strengths, and weaknesses of the seven churches are dealt with in chapters 2 and 3.

"WHO IS WORTHY?"

In chapter 4 John brings us to the vision of one sitting on a throne in heaven. Around the throne were twenty four elders clothed in white, and on their heads were crowns of gold (v.2,4). In chapter 5, we read that John "saw in the right hand of him that sat on the throne a book written within and on the backside, sealed with seven seals" (v.1). In other words, the book was completely sealed.

An angel asks with a loud voice, "Who is worthy to open the book, and to loose the seals thereof?" (v.2).

John reveals that "no man in heaven, nor on earth, nor under the earth, was able to open the book, or look thereon" (v.3). John "wept much because no man was found worthy to open and read the book, neither to look thereon" (v.4).

At this juncture one of the elders said to John: "Weep not: behold, the Lion of the Tribe of Juda, the Root of David [Jesus, *Isaiah* 11:10] has prevailed to open the book, and to loose the seven seals thereof...." [Jesus Christ, alone, was able to completely reveal that which was sealed].

"And they sung a new song, saying, You are worthy to take the book, and to open the seals thereof: **for** you were slain, **and have redeemed [purchased] us to God by your blood** out of **every** kindred, and tongue, and people, and nation.

"And **have** [present tense] made **us** unto our God kings and priests, and we shall reign upon the earth" (vs.9,10).

The Apostle Peter fills in additional details. To first century Christians, he wrote: "But you **are** [present tense] a chosen generation, a royal priesthood, an holy nation, a peculiar people; that you should show forth the praises of him [Christ] who **has called you out of** darkness **into** his most marvelous light" (*I Peter* 2:9). It is crucial that we understand that Christ came to "save his people **from** [not in] their sins" (*Matthew* 1:21). The word "from" means "out of, and away from. Distance."

THE LIGHT OF THE WORLD

During his earthly ministry, Jesus Christ was "the light of the world" (*John* 8:12). Now, through God's grace and the indwelling power of the Holy Spirit, his disciples are "the light of the world" (*Matthew* 5:14). Jesus commanded: "Let your light so shine before men, that they may **see** your good works [**not, hear your good words!**], and glorify your Father which is in heaven" (*Matthew* 5:16). Because of their calling and redemption, his disciples are also "the salt of the earth" — they add flavor to their environment (*Matthew* 5:13). They also have a purifying and preserving effect on the otherwise decaying society around them. Christ "gave himself **for** us that he might redeem us **from** all iniquity, and **purify** unto himself a peculiar people zealous of good works" (*Titus* 2:14).

The word "peculiar" in the Hebrew and Greek languages (Strong's references, #4041 and #5459) means, "gather or accumulate, peculiar treasure, special." God's "peculiar people" are, therefore, those whom God has gathered or accumulated (through redemption by the blood of Christ) from "every kindred, and tongue, and people, and nation" (*Revelation* 5:9). They are his special treasure. As we saw previously, they are also "a chosen generation, a royal priesthood, an holy nation, a peculiar people."

The New Testament Israel of God (*Galatians* 6:16) is a **spiritual** organism — "an holy temple in the Lord ... an habitation of God through the spirit" (*Ephesians* 2:22). It is the counterpart to **physical** Israel of the Old Testament. In their own time and place, they were both God's "peculiar treasure" and "peculiar people" (*Psalm* 135:4 and *Deuteronomy* 14:2).

DEFICIENCY IN THE PEOPLE

In Old Testament times the inability of the people to obey God didn't result from a deficiency in his law; rather, it lay with a deficiency in the people. In their carnal minded, rebellious, and Satan-deceived fallen state, they were just physically incapable of obeying God (*Romans* 8:7).

They needed a Redeemer. They needed a Savior.

"For what the law could **not** do, in that **it was weak through the flesh,** God sending his own son in the likeness of sinful flesh, and for sin, condemned sin in the flesh.

THE NEW TESTAMENT CHURCH

"That the righteousness of the law might be fulfilled in us who walk nor after the flesh, but after the spirit" (*Romans* 8:,3,4).

"The law was given by Moses, but grace and life came through Jesus Christ" (*John* 1:17).

"For in Adam all die, even so in Christ shall all be made alive" (*I Corinthians* 15:22). "And so it is written, The first man Adam was made a living soul; the last man Adam was made **a quickening spirit**.

"Howbeit that was not first which was spiritual, but that which is natural; and afterward that which is spiritual.

"The first man was of the earth, earthy; the second man is the Lord from heaven" (*I Corinthians* 15:45-47).

THE HUNDRED AND FORTY FOUR THOUSAND

Return now to *Revelation* 7. In the opening verse, we read that the catastrophes that were to strike the earth were to be withheld till the servants of God were "sealed ... in their foreheads" (with "the seal of the living God," v.2), v.3.

With the above facts firmly in mind, we seek the true identity of the 144,000 which John **heard** about (note that he didn't **see** this number). Here again, we see God is giving his servants a wonderfully encouraging and sustaining message. Being his servants or saints, and therefore having "ears to hear" what the spirit is saying to the churches — and being well acquainted with biblical history — the recipients were able to decipher the message loud and clear. They understood that God was talking about "the perfect church," the complete number of his servants throughout all ages (in both the Old and New Testaments).

In the Old Testament God was represented by the twelve tribes of Israel; in the first century, following the birth, crucifixion, resurrection and ascension of Jesus Christ, he was represented by the twelve disciples. Twelve multiplied by twelve = 144.

Where does the thousand come in? Throughout the Bible, the number ten is recognized as the number of finality, Again, the number 3 is recognized as the number of completion. When we multiply the number of finality (10) by the number of completion X 3, we get 10, 100, 1000. Thus, by divine mathematics, we are able to recognize the 144,000. This symbolic number represents all of the servants (or saints) of God who have ever lived, or will ever live from the creation to the very end of time. These are they whose names have been in the Lamb's book of life from before the foundation of the world (*Ephesians* 1:4; *Philippians* 4:3; *I Peter* 1:19,20, and *Revelation* 17:8); they also represent those of whom Jesus spoke when he said, "Of those which you gave me, I have lost none" (*John* 18:9).

The 144,000 pictures the perfected church which Christ purchased with his own precious blood. Complete. Perfected.

TRIBES OF ISRAEL

Verse 4 describes the 144,000 as being representative of "all the tribes of the children of Israel." But there is a difficulty here if we attempt to understand their meaning in a physical (literal) sense; the names listed are not only out of order but they do not fully correspond with the names of the twelve literal tribes listed in the Old Testament (*Genesis* 49). It is therefore unlikely that they represent the twelve physical tribes of the Old Testament.

Who, then, do they represent? When we apply the key that God gives us in *Revelation* 1:1 (that the book is primarily written in signs and symbols), we can begin to see and understand their true meaning in a very wonderful — and truly significant — way. The names of the "tribes" listed in *Revelation* 7:5-8 picture the true gospel message and the characteristics exhibited by those who are the chosen of God; the meaning of the names describe the attributes of the church.

JUDAH

In this listing, Judah is named first in place of the physical firstborn, Reuben. Why? The name Judah means, "You are he whom your brethren shall praise" (*Genesis* 49:8). There's the answer! Jesus Christ, "the lion of the tribe of Judah" (*Revelation* 5:5), is now the one whom his brethren praise. He shed his blood for their redemption; they are saved by his life (*Romans* 5:8-10). They were "bought with a price" — his blood (*I Corinthians* 6:20). Jesus Christ is the "chief cornerstone" upon which the "household of God," the New Testament church — or the Israel of God — is built (*Ephesians* 2:20, *Galatians* 6:6). He, alone, is "the way, the truth, and the life" (*John* 14:6); he is also "the Alpha and Omega, the beginning and the end" of all things (*Revelation* 1:8). He is "King or kings, and Lord of lords" (*II Timothy* 6:15; *Revelation* 17:14, 19:16).

God's word firmly establishes Jesus Christ as "the firstborn among many brethren" (*Romans* 8:29). He is "the firstborn of every creature" (*Colossians* 1:15). He "is the head of the body, the church: who is the beginning, the firstborn from the dead; that in all things he might have preeminence" (*Colossians* 1:18).

As Christ is "the firstborn" spiritually, he naturally is placed before Reuben, who was the firstborn physically.

REUBEN

Continuing with the names of the "tribes" listed in *Revelation* 7, we now come to the second name listed, Reuben. The meaning of his name is, "Behold a son." These are the sons of God, the brothers and sisters of Christ. "Behold, what manner of love the Father has bestowed upon us, that we should be called the sons of God..." (*I John* 3:1). "For as many as are led by the Spirit of God, they are the sons of God" (*Romans* 8:14).

GAD

The third name listed is Gad. His name means, "A great company." The 144,000 is made up of a great company of many sons. As they are Christ's, they are Abraham's seed and numbered "as the stars of heaven" and "as the dust of the earth" (*Galatians* 3:29).

ASER (ASHER)

Aser is the fourth name listed. His name means "joy filled." Joy is one of the fruits of the Holy Spirits (*Galatians* 5:22). It was something that characterized the church in the first century.

During a lengthy and detailed talk to his disciples (*John*, chapters 14-17), Jesus said he was speaking to them "that my joy might remain in you, and that your joy might be full" (15:11). It was Christ's prayer that his joy should be "fulfilled" in the church (17:13). The Apostle Paul records that Jesus' disciples "were filled with joy and with the Holy Spirit" (*Acts* 13:52).

In fact, "The kingdom of God is ... righteousness, and peace, and joy in the Holy Spirit" (*Romans* 14:17).

NEPHTHALIM

The fifth name, Nephthalim, means to "wrestle and overcome."

The body of Christ is made up of those who wrestle "against principalities, against powers, against the rulers of darkness of this world, against spiritual wickedness [or, wicked spirits] in high places" (*Ephesians* 6:12). In addition, they wrestle against the world — "the lust of the flesh, the lust of the eyes, and the pride of life" (*I John* 2:15-16). Through the power of the Holy Spirit, they are overcomers (*Romans* 12:21; *I John* 2:13-14, *I John* 4:4).

MANASSES

The sixth name, Manasses, means "Forgetting." As a result of having been raised to newness of life through the indwelling power of the risen Christ, they have forgotten the bondage of sin. "As far as the east is from the west, so far has he [God] removed our transgressions from us" (*Psalm* 103:12).

"[F]orgetting those things which are behind, and reaching forth unto those things which are before, I press toward the mark for the prize of the high calling of God in Christ Jesus" (*Philippians* 3:13-14).

SIMEON

The seventh name, Simeon, means "Hearing." These are the people who have heard the call of God. As Jesus said: "My sheep **hear** my voice, and I know them, and they follow me" (*John* 10:27). By the Sovereign grace of God, they have been given "**ears to hear**" the call of God.

LEVI

The eighth name, Levi, means "Joined." These are the people who are joined to the Lord by the Holy Spirit. In their personal lives they bring forth the fruit of that spirit: "love, joy, peace, longsuffering, gentleness, goodness, faith, meekness, temperance: against such there is no law" (*Galatians* 6:22).

ISSACHAR

The ninth name, Issachar, means "A price was paid." These are those who have been redeemed by the blood of Jesus Christ; he paid the price for their sins on the cross. In the words of an old hymn: "We owed a debt we could not pay; He paid a debt he did not owe."

ZABULON (ZEBULON)

The tenth name, Zabulon, means "A dwelling place." The Bible clearly reveals that Christians are the "dwelling place" of God through the spirit.

"Now therefore **you** are no more strangers and foreigners, but fellow citizens with the saints, and of the household of God.

"And are built up upon the foundation of the apostles and prophets, Jesus Christ himself being the chief corner stone;

"In whom all the building fitly framed together groweth into a holy temple in the Lord:

"**In whom you also are builded together for a habitation [dwelling place] of God through the Spirit**" (*Ephesians* 2:19-22).

"Don't you know that you are the temple of God, and that the Spirit of God dwells in you? (*I Corinthians* 3:16).

These are "a chosen [**not choosing!**] generation, a royal priesthood, a holy nation, a peculiar people; that you should show forth the praises of him who has **called** you out of darkness into his most marvelous light:

"Which in time past were not a people, but are now the people of God: which had not obtained mercy, but now have obtained mercy" (*I Peter* 2:9-10).

JOSEPH

The eleventh name, Joseph, means "A fruitful bow ... by a well; whose branches run over the wall" (Genesis 49:22). These are the people who produce the fruit of the Holy Spirit in their lives. Their branches reach out to the people of other nations so that they, too, may partake of the blessings of God.

"If you be Christ's, then are you Abraham's seed, and heirs according to the promise" (*Galatians* 3:29).

BENJAMIN

Finally, the twelfth name, Benjamin (Benoni): "Son of my sorrow" — "son of (the father's) right hand" (*Strong's Exhaustive Concordance*, references #1126 and #1144).

This twelfth name concludes the list "of all the tribes of the children of Israel" (*Revelation* 7:4) by pointing back once again to Jesus Christ, who is "the Alpha and Omega, the beginning [Judah] and the ending [Benjamin]" (*Revelation* 1:8).

As prophesied some 750 years before his birth, Jesus was certainly "despised and rejected of men; **a man of sorrows**, and acquainted with grief: and we hid as it were our faces from him; **he was despised**, and we esteemed him not" (*Isaiah* 53:3).

How was this fulfilled in the New Testament? "And when he was come near [Jerusalem], he beheld the city, and wept over it" (*Luke* 19:41). Why? He was just about to spell out Jerusalem's doom in no uncertain terms (vs.42-44). As Jesus neared his crucifixion, he also declared, "My soul is exceeding sorrowful even unto death" (*Matthew* 26:38).

The people "esteemed him not"? "He came unto his own and his own received him not" (*John* 1:11).

Despised? "[T]hey spit in his face and buffeted him; and others smote him with the palms of their hands" (*Matthew* 26:67).

Also, as pointed out earlier, Benjamin means "son of (the father's) right hand" (*Strong's*, #1144). This is undeniably borne out in the life of Christ: "[H]e was received up into heaven, and sat on the right hand of God" (*Mark* 16:19). He "is even at the right hand of God ... [and] maketh intercession for us" (*Romans* 8:34). Through the words of a prophetic psalm, God said to Christ: "Sit you on my right hand, till I make your enemies your footstool" (*Matthew* 22:44; *Psalm* 110:1).

Jesus Christ began it; Jesus Christ will finish it. "All things were made by him [the Word, who became Jesus]. And without him was not anything made that was made" (*John* 1:3). "Then comes the end, when he shall have delivered up the kingdom to God, even the Father; when he shall have put down all rule, and all authority and power.

"For he must reign till he has put all enemies under his feet.

"The last enemy that shall be destroyed is death" (*I Corinthians* 15:24-26). "For the Father ... has committed all judgment unto the Son" (*John* 5:22).

THEY ARE "SEALED"

Notice, also, that the 144,000 are "**sealed**." What does this mean? The Apostle Paul tells us that "the son of God, Jesus Christ [in whom are all the promises of God] ... has "**sealed** us, and given us the earnest [down payment] of the Holy Spirit of promises" (*II Corinthians* 1:22. Also vs.19,20. Reference, *Galatians* 3:29).

In *Ephesians* 1:13, Paul elaborates: "In whom [Christ, v.10] you also trusted, after that you heard the word of truth, the gospel of your salvation; in whom also after you believed, you were **sealed** with that holy Spirit of promise.

"Which is the earnest of your salvation, until the redemption of the purchased possession, unto the praise of his glory."

What is the inheritance of those who are sealed? With Abraham, they "look for a city which has foundations, whose builder and maker is God" (*Hebrews* 11:10). More on this later.

WHY NO "DAN"?

Why is Dan not listed among "**all** the tribes of Israel" mentioned in *Revelation* 7? The reason appears to rest in the meaning of the name: Dan means "God has judged me." The people who make up the symbolic 144,000 are no longer under the judgment of God. The penalty of their sins was paid by Jesus on the cross. "[T]he blood of Jesus Christ ... cleanses us from all sin" (*I John* 1:7). "There is therefore no condemnation to them which are in Christ Jesus, who walk not after the flesh, but after the spirit"(*Romans* 8:1).

Jesus said: "Verily, verily, I say unto you, He that hears my words [his sheep, *John* 10:27], and believes on him that sent me, has everlasting life, and shall not come into condemnation, but is passed from death unto life" (*John* 5:24).

COMPLETE ISRAEL OF GOD

In their totality, these 144,000 represent the true and complete Israel of God (*Galatians* 6:16). As they are "Christ's, then are [they] Abraham's seed, and heirs according to the promise" (*Galatians* 3:29). As the name Israel implies, they are people who have been truly "conquered by God." They are the **chosen** people.

As Jesus stated: "You have not chosen me, but I have chosen you, and ordained you, that you should go and bring forth fruit, and that your fruit should remain, that whatsoever you ask the Father in my name, he may give it you.

"These things I command you, that you love one another.

"If the world hate you, you know that it hated me before it hated you.

"If you were of the world, the world would love his own; but because you are not of the world, but I have chosen you out of the world, therefore the world hateth you.

"Remember the word that I said unto you, The servant is not greater than his lord. If they have persecuted me, they will also persecute you; if they have kept my sayings, they will keep your's also" (*John* 15:16-20).

A GREAT MULTITUDE WHICH NO MAN COULD NUMBER

The belief that the hundred and forty-four thousand (the number John **heard**) is symbolic or figurative — and not a literal number relating to the 12 physical tribes of Israel — is further borne out in *Revelation* by a scripture that appears just a few verses later. This relates to what John **saw**: "After this, I saw, and lo, a great multitude, which no man could number, of all nations, and kindreds, and people, and tongues, stood before the throne, and before the Lamb, clothed with white robes, and palms in their hands" *(Revelatlion* 7:9).

"What are these, which are arrayed in white robes, and whence came they?...

"These are they which came out of great tribulation, and have washed their robes, and made them white in the blood of the Lamb" (*Revelation* 7:13-14).

Note that John only **heard** the symbolic number, but that he **saw** the "great multitude which no man, could number." They are one and the same.

"THEY ARE VIRGINS"

The 144,00 are also pictured in *Revelation* 14: "And they sung as it were a new song, before the throne, and before the four beasts, and the elders: and no man could learn that song but the hundred and forty four thousand, which are **redeemed** from the earth.

"These are they which were not defiled by women; for they are virgins. These are they which follow the Lamb wherever he goes. These are **redeemed** from among men, being the **firstfruits** unto God, and to the Lamb.

"And in their mouth was found no guile: for they are without fault before the throne of God" (*Revelation* 14:3-5). Like Nathaniel, they were "Israelites indeed" — true spiritual Israel (*John* 1:47).

Notice particularly verse 4: "They are not defiled with women ... they are virgins." Obviously, as God condones marriage, this can hardly be taken in a physical sense: "Marriage is honorable, and the bed undefiled: but whoremongers and adulterers will God judge (*Hebrews* 13:4).

We should therefore look for another explanation — one that is more completely in line with Scripture. In the Old Testament we read about ancient Israel being married to God (*Ezekiel* 16). We are told that, **in the spiritual sense**, physical Israel "went a whoring after other gods, and bowed themselves to them: they turned quickly out of the way" (*Judges* 2:17). Israel "went a whoring after the gods of the people of the land, whom God destroyed before them" (*I Chronicles* 5:25). "The spirit of whoredoms ... caused them to err; and they [went] a whoring from under their God" (*Hosea* 4:12). Yes, Israel "played the harlot ... opening her feet [legs] to every one that passed by, and multiplied [her] whoredoms" (*Ezekiel* 16:25).

Here we see from scripture that most people in ancient Israel were spiritual whores — not spiritual virgins.

THE GREAT WHORE

Now, back to the New Testament. Continuing in the "Revelation of Jesus Christ," John was instructed: "Come here, and I will show you the judgement of the great whore that sits upon many waters" (*Revelation* 17:1). Verse 15 tells us that the "many waters ... **are** peoples and multitudes, and nations, and tongues."

Notice that world leaders have "committed fornication" with the great whore, and that "the inhabitants of the earth have been made drunk with the wine of her fornications" (v.2).

In *Strong's*, #4202 - 4205, "fornication" is defined as "harlotry (including adultery and incest); fig. idolatry; fornication."

By a secular source it is defined as: "Voluntary sexual intercourse between a man (strictly, an unmarried man) and an unmarried woman. In Scripture, extended to adultery. b. *fig*. The forsaking of God for idols, idolatry" (*The Oxford Universal Dictionary*).

BABYLON THE GREAT

This woman, the great whore, had a name on her forehead: "MYSTERY, BABYLON THE GREAT, THE MOTHER OF HARLOTS AND ABOMINATIONS OF THE EARTH.

"And I saw the woman drunken with the blood of the saints, and with the blood of the martyrs of Jesus...." (vs.5,6).

Here we see a picture of the great religious system which originated in Nimrod's Babylon. It is a worldwide system which has deceived and corrupted all nations. The great whore hates God and his truth, and is out to eliminate the true people of God (the saints) from the face of the earth.

Notice also that the great whore has daughters; these came out of her (in Protest?) and are part of the same corrupt system. Under their true master, Satan (who appears as "an angel of light," *II Corinthians* 11:14), they have deceived the whole world — spiritually and politically — and turned it into a state of total confusion. (Babylon the Great means "Great Confusion").

As thoroughly documented in such books as Alexander Hislop's *Two Babylons* and this writer's *Fourth Reich of the Rich*, the same religious system has come down to us in the form of the Roman Catholic church and the other churches which came out of her at the time of the Protestant Reformation.

THE VIRGINS ARE THE ELECT

The "virgins" pictured in chapter 14 are the "elect" or "remnant" of God — the ones whom God has chosen from before the foundation of the earth. They have, by the grace of God, "been reconciled to God by the death of his son" (*Romans* 5:10), and, by the power of the Holy Spirit, raised to newness of life in Christ Jesus. "God ... even when we were dead in sins, has quickened us [made us alive] together with Christ (by grace you are saved).

"And has raised us up together, and made us sit together in heavenly places in Christ Jesus" (*Ephesians* 2:4,5,6).

Why? "That he might present it to himself as a glorious church, not having spot or wrinkle, or any such thing; but that it should be holy and without blemish" (*Ephesians* 5:27). "Though your sins be scarlet, they shall be white as snow" (*Isaiah* 1:18).

"How much more shall the blood of Christ ... purge your conscience from dead works to serve the living God" (*Hebrews* 9:14).

Obviously, if the 144,000 (or the complete true church) is without "spot or wrinkle" and "holy and without blemish," its members may be rightly classified as spiritual virgins. That ties in perfectly with the

Apostle Paul's declared objective of presenting disciples "as ... chaste virgin[s] to Christ" (*II Corinthians* 11:2).

These are they who are the virgin Bride of Christ: "Praise your God, all you his servants [those to whom the Revelation was given, 1:1], and you that fear him, both small and great.

"And I heard as it were the voice of a great multitude [the saints, 7:9], and as the voice of many waters, and as the voice of many thunderings, saying, **Alleluia, for the Lord God omnipotent reigns**.

"Let us be glad and rejoice, and give honor to him: for the marriage of the Lamb is come, and his wife has made herself ready.

"And to her was **granted** that she **should be** arrayed in fine linen, clean and white: **for the fine linen is the righteousness of the saints**. [Notice it was granted to her. "By grace are you saved through faith ... and that **not** of yourselves: it is the gift of God.]

"Not of works, lest any man should boast" (*Ephesians* 2:8,9)].

"And he said unto me, Write, Blessed are they which are **called** unto the marriage supper of the Lamb.... These are the true sayings of God (*Revelation* 19:5-9).

Readers will notice that this scene is the exact opposite to that pictured in *Ezekiel*, chapter 16. In that Old Testament passage, God divorced "whorish" physical Israel. At the end of the New Testament, he marries spiritual Israel, the church.

"Moreover, whom he did predestinate, them he also called: and whom he called, them he also justified: and whom he justified, them he also glorified" (*Romans* 8:30).

Chapter 16

The New Covenant And The 70 Weeks Prophecy

The subject of the New Covenant is one that is basically ignored in most churches today; it is a subject referred to only fleetingly, if at all. Over the years, this writer can only remember having heard two pastors address the issue in any depth. It is almost as if it were a forbidden topic; the reason for this will emerge later in this chapter.

The phrase "New Covenant" appears in only four places in the Bible — once in the Old Testament, *Jeremiah* 31:31, and three times in the New Testament, *Hebrews* 8:8; 8:13, and 12:24. Under the term, "New Testament," it appears 6 times (*Matthew* 26:28; *Mark* 14:24; *Luke* 22:20; *I Corinthians* 11:25; *II Corinthians* 3:6, and *Hebrews* 9:15). A lack of knowledge and understanding in the church regarding the vital nature of this subject is one of the main reasons why there is a lack of spiritual vitality at this crucial time in world history.

To gain a clearer overview of what the New Covenant is all about, we need to start off at the first place it appears in Scripture:

"Behold the days come, says the Lord, that I will make **a new covenant** with the house of Israel, and with the house of Judah:

THE NEW COVENANT AND THE 70 WEEKS PROPHECY

"**Not** according to the covenant that I made with their fathers in the day that I brought them out of the land of Egypt; **which covenant they broke** although I was an husband unto them, says the Lord.

"But **this** is the covenant that **I** shall make with the house of Israel; after those days, says the Lord, **I** will put **my** law in their inward parts, **and** write it in their hearts; **and** will be **their God, and** they shall be **my people**.

"And they shall teach no more every man his neighbor and every man his brother saying, Know the Lord: for they shall **all** know me, from the least of them unto the greatest of them, says the Lord; for **I** will forgive their iniquity, and **I** will remember their sin no more" (*Jeremiah* 31:31-34).

"MY PEOPLE"

Notice that only the people involved in the New Covenant have the true God as "their God" — thus becoming "my people." Logic dictates that, as they "were dead in [their] tresspasses and sins" (*Ephesians* 2:1), he was not their God, and that they are not "his people" **prior** to the ratification of that covenant — and their calling. Now, notice the words "house of Israel" and "house of Judah" in verse 31; this is reduced to the collective "house of Israel" in verse 33. The meaning of the two names is significant: Judah means "praise," and Israel means "conquered by God." It appears, then, that the New Covenant is made with those who — being conquered by God — give him all the praise and glory. They are now "the Israel of God" (*Galatians* 6:16).

SOVEREIGN GRACE

The first thing we need to notice about the New Covenant, as expressed in the word of God, is the fact that it reveals to us, more than 600 years before Christ, what God — in his sovereign grace — is going to do. It says **absolutely nothing** about any participation by mortal man in the drawing up or ratification of the Covenant. It is exclusively the work of the Sovereign God: "I shall.... I will...."

The New Covenant is not like other covenants that God made with man; the problem in previous covenants was **not** with God — it was with man (*Hebrews* 8:7,8). Because of his sinful nature (*Romans* 8:7), man was unable to keep them; he violated and broke every one of them.

This was not going to happen again.

Notice again what God says: "**I** will put **my** law in their inward parts, **and** write it in their hearts; **and** will be their God, **and** they shall be my people.... I will forgive their iniquity, and I will remember their sin no more."

Notice something else of tremendous importance in this prophecy by Jeremiah: "**[T]hey shall all know me, from the least of them unto the greatest of them, says the Lord.**"

In theological terminology, the word "know" (or "knew") means to have a close, intimate relationship with someone. For example: "Adam knew his wife, and she conceived." Also, "Cain knew his wife, and she conceived" (*Genesis* 4:1,17). This concept is further elaborated upon in *Genesis* 4:25; 18:19; 19:5; 42:7. Also, *Exodus* 1:8.

The question now arises, How can mortal man, who is "dead in trespasses and sins" (*Ephesians* 2:1), come to have a close, intimate relationship with his Creator? Obviously, he can't — unless something totally supernatural occurs. That "something" is, of course, the intervention of God in the person of Jesus Christ: "For **by grace** are you saved, through faith; and that **not** of yourselves: it is the **gift** of God.

"**Not** by works, **lest** any man should boast" (*Ephesians* 2:9,10).

Have the wonderful things God promised to do for the new Israel under the terms of the New Covenant been already accomplished, or are they on hold till some unspecified, future time? Was the New Covenant confirmed by Christ in the first century — or must we wait till some future date for its ratification? The confusion has arisen — much to the detriment of many sincere followers, or would-be followers of Jesus Christ — as a result of the misunderstanding of a crucial prophecy in the book of Daniel. Let's check it out.

THE SEVENTY WEEKS PROPHECY

Daniel was a captive in Babylon following king Nebuchadnezzar's conquest of Judah. The theme of his book is the sovereignty of God over the affairs of men in all ages. In chapter 9, Daniel tells of an encounter he had with Gabriel, who is elsewhere identified as an angelic messenger of God (*Luke* 1:19,26; *Daniel* 8:16).

Gabriel said: "I am now come forth to **give** you skill and understanding.... I am come to **show** you; for you are greatly beloved; **therefore understand the matter**, and consider the vision.

"Seventy weeks are determined upon your people and upon your holy city, to [1] **finish the transgressions**, and to [2] **make an end of sins**, and to [3] **make reconciliation for iniquity**, and to [4] **bring in everlasting righteousness**, and to [5] **seal up the vision and prophecy**, and to [6] **anoint the most Holy**" (*Daniel* 9:21,22-24).

"**Know** therefore and **understand**, that **from** the going forth of the commandment to restore and build Jerusalem, **unto the Messiah the Prince** shall be seven weeks, and three score and two weeks: the street shall be built again, and the wall even in troublous times" (v.25).

"And after three score and two weeks shall Messiah be cut off, but **not** for himself: and the people of the prince shall come and destroy the city and the sanctuary; and the end thereof shall be with a flood, and unto the end of the war desolations are determined" (v.26).

"And he shall confirm the covenant with many for one week, and in the midst of the week he shall cause the sacrifice and oblation to cease and for the overspreading of abomination he shall make it desolate, even unto the consummation, and **that determined** shall be poured out upon the desolate" (v.27).

FULFILLMENT

Particularly in the twentieth century a great deal of confusion has existed regarding the fulfillment of this vital prophecy. As the result of starting off with a false premise (an erroneous assumption), most writers on the subject have reached conclusions that are detrimental to the spiritual well-being of their readers. The confusion is centered primarily on their misinterpretation of certain stated facts.

These authors have two main problems: (1) What was the date of "the going forth of the commandment to restore and rebuild Jerusalem"? (this would mark the beginning of the seventy weeks), and (2) Is the seventy weeks one single span of time, or is it divided up into dispensations?

When attempting to determine the date of the command by king Cyrus of Persia to rebuild Jerusalem (as recorded in *Ezra* 1:1-4 and *II Chronicles* 36:22-23, and prophesied 200 years earlier in *Isaiah* 44:24,26-28), most modern writers have relied almost exclusively on sources that can only lead to erroneous conclusions. The majority have relied upon *Ussher's Chronology of the Bible*, which was developed by James Ussher, Archbishop of Armagh, Ireland nearly four hundred years ago.

For many years *Ussher's Chronology* was one of the faulty building blocks upon which such men as Ethelbert W. Bullinger and Cyrus I. Scofield based their interpretations of such biblical passages as *Daniel* 9:25-27. Unfortunately for the unsuspecting people who innocently accepted their interpretation as "gospel," Ussher's work was **not** based exclusively on the Bible; instead, it relied heavily upon other, unsubstantiated sources such as Ptolemy's table of Persian kings. As a result, it was off by some eighty years. In essence, apart from the Bible there is no chronology in existence for the period in question.

MARTIN ANSTEY

In the modern era, the full truth only came to light when, in 1913, Martin Anstey published his *Bible Chronology*. Anstey's system of chronology is of inestimable value because it is based exclusively on the biblical record; as such, it can be verified by all Bible students. As a result, the errors pertaining to the understanding of the Seventy Weeks prophecy — promoted first by Bullinger, then by Scofield, and more recently by Hal Lindsey, Jack van Impe et. al. — were fully exposed. Unfortunately, even now, virtually all the modern Pop Prophets of Babylon — the vast multitude of self-professed Bible teachers whose ministries dominate the TV and radio scene today — continue to promote the same errors.

It is a regrettable fact that Scofield and his motley offspring — despite the havoc they have wrought through the promulgation of their non-biblical, highly destructive Dispensationalist dogma — are still honored and revered in most fundamentalist circles. The scholarly work of Martin Anstey is forgotten by all but a few. Another sad reflection on the shallowness of the age in which we live!

It is an even more regrettable fact that multiple millions of church-goers pay much more attention to the footnotes in their Scofield "bibles" than they do to the actual recorded word of God.[5]

---

[5] For those who wish to learn more about the non-Christian, non-biblical lifestyle led by the chief proponent of biblically-heretical Dispensationalism, we recommend *The Incredible Scofield*, by Joseph M. Canfield. It's available from Emissary Publications.

SETTING THE DATES

According to the prophecy in Daniel, the time between the command given by Cyrus and the appearance of Messiah the Prince "**shall be** seven weeks, and threescore [60] and two weeks" — a total 69 weeks, or 483 days. On the biblical basis of a day representing a year, the total length between the two events would therefore be 483 years.

In his book, Anstey demonstrates — exclusively from scripture — the great care that God took in preserving both the date that the command went out and the date Messiah the Prince appeared. In essence, the former was "in **the first year of Cyrus king of Persia**" (*Ezra* 1:1-4); the latter was "in **the fifteenth year of Tiberius Caesar**, Pontius Pilate being governor of Judea, and Herod being tetrarch of Galilee ... [with] Annas and Caiaphas being the high priests" (*Luke* 3:1,2,21,22). Using Bible chronology exclusively, we find that the space between the two events was exactly 483 years.

It is important to note that, prior to his human birth, the One who became Jesus was known as "the Word" (*John* 1:1-5). He was only revealed as Messiah (**the Anointed One**, or the Christ) following his baptism in the River Jordan in 26 A.D. (Jesus was born in 4 B.C.).

THE SEVENTIETH WEEK

Having determined that "Messiah the Prince" came exactly 483 years after Cyrus issued his command that Jerusalem be rebuilt, we now come to the vitally important 70th week. As no biblical evidence exists for belief in a division (or mystery dispensation during which "the clock of prophecy was stopped") between the 69th and 70th week, common sense dictates that the 70th week followed immediately after the 69th week. That's why it's known as the 70th week, and not by some other designation!

The only question that now needs to be asked — and answered — is: Did the events prophesied to occur in the 70th week actually occur in the years immediately following the anointing of Messiah the Prince at the River Jordan — thus completely fulfilling the prophecy given to Daniel by Gabriel?

As a brief reminder of what we are looking for, we repeat *Daniel* 9:24: "Seventy weeks **are** determined [marked out in full], upon your people and upon your holy city, [1] to **finish the transgressions**, and to [2] **make an end of sins**, and [3] to **make reconciliation for iniquity**, and to [4] **bring in everlasting righteousness**, and to [5]

seal up the vision and prophecy, and to [6] **anoint the most Holy.**"

Part one relates to Daniel's people, these Jews, and to what was known at that time as "the holy city," Jerusalem. What was the vision and prophecy that was to be sealed up (or wrapped up) within the time determined? Verse 26 provides the answer: "**[T]he people of** the prince will come that shall destroy the city and the sanctuary; and the end thereof shall be as a flood, and unto the end of the war are desolations determined." This prophecy was dramatically fulfilled when General Vespasian (9-79 A.D.) — who had laid siege to Jerusalem in the late 60s A.D. — was called back to Rome in 69 A.D. to be made Emperor. His son, Titus — who thus became a prince — took over the siege. The following year, because of the atrocities perpetrated against the population of Jerusalem by their fellow Jews, "the people of the prince" (Titus' soldiers) proceeded to "destroy the city and the sanctuary." Jewish historian Josephus records that their actions were in direct violation of Titus' orders; he wanted to preserve both the city and the sanctuary. What an amazing fulfillment of just one small aspect of a prophecy made hundreds of years previously! The terms of the prophecy forbid its application to a future time or personage.

During the war with Rome Judea was laid totally desolate. As foretold by Jesus, upon that generation came "all the righteous blood shed" in past generations (*Matthew* 23. Read the whole chapter, but especially verses, 32, 35-38). In the seige of Jerusalem, a time of "great tribulation," 90 percent of the population was wiped out; the remaining 10 percent were dragged off into captivity. As this represents 100 percent casualties, there could never be a greater "tribulation" (*Matthew* 24:21).

How about the other aspects of this prophecy? Let's check.

"ANOINT THE MOST HOLY"?

Who is the most Holy — and when was he anointed? For the answer we go, once more, to the Bible:

When Jesus was "about thirty years of age" he was baptized in the River Jordan. Immediately afterwards, the "Holy Spirit descended in a bodily shape upon him, and a voice came from heaven, which said, You are my beloved Son; in you I am well pleased" (*Luke* 3:22,23).

In the next chapter, we read of "Jesus being full of the Holy Spirit [as he] returned from Jordan, and was led by the Spirit into the wilderness" to be tempted by the devil for 40 days (*Luke* 4:1,2). Following his defeat of Satan, as described in an earlier chapter, "Jesus returned in the power of the Spirit into Galilee." When he reached Nazareth he went into the synagogue. There, standing up to read and being given the book of Isaiah, **"he** found the place where it was written.

"The spirit of the Lord is upon me, because **he has anointed me** to preach to the poor; **he** has sent me to heal the brokenhearted, to preach deliverance to the captives, and recovering of sight to the blind, to set at liberty them that are bruised,

"To preach the acceptable year of the Lord"

When he closed the book and had sat down, he said: **"This day is this scripture fulfilled in your ears"** (*Luke* 4:18-19; also *Isaiah* 61:1).

The Apostle Paul confirmed that **"God anointed Jesus of Nazareth with the Holy Spirit and with power"** (*Acts* 10:38)

Jesus is clearly the "anointed" — Christ — mentioned in Daniel. Even the demons acknowledged that Jesus of Nazareth was "the Holy One of God" (*Luke* 4:34).

Jesus Christ's personal ministry lay entirely within the 70th week. The fact that Messiah was to be "cut off, but not for himself" in the midst of the 70th week (*Daniel* 9:27), definitely places Christ's whole ministry within the seventieth consecutive week from the decree of Cyrus. Christ, who was sinless, was "cut off" [crucified] not for himself but for the sins of others.

RECONCILIATION FOR INIQUITY?

Were people reconciled to God during this same period of time? Bearing in mind that Jesus was prophesied to "save his people from their sins" (*Matthew* 1:21), the Bible provides us with the answer: "[W]e **were** reconciled to God by the death of his Son" (*Romans* 5:10).

"God ... **has** reconciled us unto himself by Jesus Christ, and has given us the ministry of reconciliation." And again, **"God was in Christ, reconciling the world unto himself,** not imputing their trespasses unto them; **and has committed unto us the word of reconciliation"** (*II Corinthians* 5:18,19).

Jesus was, in fact, the ultimate High Priest. Unlike the high priests of old, Jesus — "who is holy, harmless, undefiled, separate from sinners, and made higher than the heavens ... entered in **once** into the holy place, **having obtained** eternal redemption for us." He "entered into heaven itself, **now** to appear in the presence of God for us." He is a "**merciful and faithful high priest** in things pertaining to God, **to make reconciliating for the sins of the people**" (*Hebrews* 7:26; 9:12; 9:24; 2:17).

"In [Christ] we have redemption through his blood, even the forgiveness of sins....

"And, **having made** peace through the blood of his cross, by him to **reconcile** all things unto himself....

"And you, that were sometime alienated and enemies in your mind by wicked works, **yet now has he reconciled**" (*Colossians* 1:14,20,-21).

"(W)e also joy in God through our **Lord Jesus Christ, by whom we have now received the atonement** [reconciliation to, or "at one ment" with God] (*Romans* 5:11)].

As Jesus' life was worth more than the lives of all the people who have ever lived, on the cross he represented the ultimate (final) sacrifice for sin. "Wherefore he **is** able also to save them to the uttermost that come to God by him, **seeing that he ever lives to make intercession for them**" (*Hebrews* 7:25).

Because of Christ, his disciples — having been reconciled to God — are now "holy brethren, partakers of the heavenly calling" (*Hebrews* 3:1).

DID JESUS "BRING IN EVERLASTING RIGHTEOUSNESS"?

Did Jesus Christ "bring in everlasting righteousness"? He certainly did! During his earthly ministry, he preached "the kingdom of heaven." He stated: "The time is fulfilled, and the kingdom of heaven is **at hand**" (*Mark* 1:14,15). He admonished his disciples to, "Seek ... first the kingdom of God **and his righteousness**" (*Matthew* 6:33). The fact that this kingdom was established shortly thereafter (following his death, resurrection, and ascension) is demonstrated by Paul's statement that "the kingdom of God **is** [present tense] ... righteousness and peace, and joy **in the Holy Spirit**" (*Romans* 14:17).

One aspect of God's **righteousness**, which he was to "bring in" through the sacrifice of Christ (*Romans* 3:21-26), is that it is eternal or **everlasting** (see also *Isaiah* 51:8). That righteousness is now applied to those who are "in Christ Jesus" (*I Corinthians* 1:30). All the glory for this must be given to the Lord (v.31).

One result of everlasting righteousness is everlasting life. "Verily, verily, I say unto you, He that hears my word, and believes on him that sent me, **has** [present tense] **everlasting life**, and shall **not** come into condemnation; but **is passed** from death unto life" (*John* 5:24). As another scripture states: "There is therefore now **no condemnation** to them which are in Christ, who walk not after the flesh but after the Spirit" (*Romans* 8:1). Of course! They have been reconciled to God through Christ.

"Verily, verily, I say unto you, He that believes on me **has everlasting life**" (*John* 6:47).

"[O]ur Savior Jesus Christ, who **has** [present tense] abolished death, and **has** brought life and immortality to light through the gospel" (*II Timothy* 1:10).

SEAL UP THE VISION AND PROPHECY?

As a result of what occurred in 70 A.D., the vision and prophecy given to Daniel by Gabriel were sealed up — or wrapped up — during the "determined" period of time. Everything prophesied to happen within the 70 weeks was fulfilled. These events also brought to completion the Abrahamic covenant which God had made with physical Israel. It was Israel that broke the covenant; as a result — and as prophesied — they were totally destroyed (*Deuteronomy* 28. Read the whole chapter, but particularly verse 53, and verses 59-67).

All prophecy is focused on and summed up in Jesus Christ: "To him give all the prophets witness" (*Acts* 10:43). As Jesus stated, his whole purpose was "to do the will of him that sent [him] and to finish his work" (*John* 4:34). On the cross, of his work he said: "It is finished" (*John* 19:30). Interestingly, the 70th week ended in 70 A.D.

JUBILEE AND NEW COVENANT

When we further break down the numbers given by Gabriel to Daniel another wonderful truth unfolds. In numbering the 70 weeks, the first part mentioned is "seven weeks" (*Daniel* 9:25). What does this mean? The Old Testament gives us the key to the explanation: "And you shall number **seven sabbaths of years unto you**, seven times seven years; **and the space of the seven sabbaths shall be**

unto you forty nine years" (*Leviticus* 25:8). The fiftieth year was extra special: "And you shall hallow the fiftieth year, and **proclaim liberty throughout all the land** unto all the inhabitants thereof; **it shall be a Jubilee unto you**; and you shall return every man unto his possession, and you shall return every man unto his family" (*Leviticus* 25:10).

On that fiftieth year all debts were forgiven, all obligations nullified; everybody started off again with a clean slate.

When we take "seven sabbaths of years, seven times seven years" (or 49 years) and multiple that number by 10 (the biblical number of completion) we come once more to 490 years — and "Messiah the Prince," or Jesus Christ. **He truly is our Jubilee, the one through whom and by whom all our debts are forgiven**. He is the one who "proclaims our liberty" by wiping our individual slates clean and allowing us to start over as new creations in him. "Though your sins be as scarlet, they shall be as white as snow; though they be red like crimson, they shall be as wool" (*Isaiah* 1:18).

"But now in Christ Jesus you who were sometimes far off are made near by the blood of Christ.

"**For he is our peace**, who has made both one, and has broken down the middle wall of partition between us;

"Having abolished in his flesh the enmity, even the law of commandments contained in ordinances; **for to make in himself of the two one new man, so making peace**;

"And that he might **reconcile both unto God in one body by the cross**, having slain the enmity thereby" (*Ephesians* 2:13-16).

NEW COVENANT RATIFIED

All this was accomplished through the ratification of the New Covenant sealed by the sacrificial shedding of Christ's blood on the cross: "**For this is my blood of the new testament [covenant], which is shed for many for the remission of sins**" (*Matthew* 26:28). As a "lamb without blemish and without spot" (*I Peter* 1:19), "Christ our passover [was] sacrificed for us" (*I Corinthians* 5:7). As such, Jesus is "the mediator of the new covenant" (*Hebrews* 12:24).

The New Covenant which is made with the New Israel of God (*Galatians* 3:29; 6:16) is totally supernatural in nature. God does all the work. God "works in you both to will and to do of his good pleasure" (*Philippians* 2:13). **He** saves **his** people **from** their sins

(*Matthew* 1:21). **He** puts **his** law in their inward parts, **and** writes it in their hearts; he is their God, **and** they are his people.

Not only has he forgiven their iniquities and remembers their sins no more, he has also given them his Holy Spirit — "the Spirit of truth and of a sound mind" (*II Timothy* 1:17). As also prophesied in *Jeremiah* 31:31-34, they all "know the Lord [have a close, intimate relationship with him] ... from the least of them unto the greatest of them."

Having a close, intimate relationship with the One who is "the way, the truth, and the life," with the One who said, "I will never leave you, nor forsake you," and the One who is "the same yesterday, and today, and forever" far transcends anything even conceivable to mortal man (*John* 14:6; *Hebrews* 13:5,8). No wonder the apostle Paul said that God's people "rejoice with joy unspeakable and full of glory" (I *Peter* 1:8). It is even less wonder that Paul said that, in comparison, everything else is "dung" (*Philippians* 3:8).

Resting in and responding to Jesus Christ as Lord, the elect of God experience "the peace of God which passes all understanding." Of course! **He is their Jubilee, their rest — their Sabbath of sabbaths.** "Where the spirit of the Lord is, there is liberty" (*II Corinthians* 3:17).

"For we which have believed do enter into rest....

"There remains therefore a rest to the people of God.

"For he that is entered into his rest, he also has ceased from his **own** works, as God did from his.

"Let us labor therefore to enter into that rest...." (*Hebrews* 4:3,9-11).

Chapter 17

The Big Showdown

What does the future hold? Will our society continue to desintegrate? Will we finally collapse in a heap of ruins? Will we ultimately be merged into a luciferian new World Order to be ruled over in a "feudalistic fashion" as predicted by President Clinton's mentor, Dr. Carroll Quigley?

When we look objectively at the world today, we must honestly admit that the Satanic powers of evil and destruction are everywhere dominant. Truth and righteousness are being trampled into the ground at every point of the compass; it appears as if they have been overwhelmed and conquered by the forces of evil.

Is there any hope that things will be turned around — or are we destined to go over the cliff ... into national oblivion?

This writer believes there can be no real confidence in the future unless we see current events through the eyes of what the Bible calls "the more sure word of prophecy" (*II Peter* 1:19). As a result, he is confident that there is a Big Showdown coming between the God of the Bible and Satan — and that God will triumph!

When this author was first introduced to the subject of Bible prophecy back in the mid-1950s, the prophet Daniel's telescopic vision regarding past, present, and future world kingdoms (*Daniel*

2:1-45) was the reference used most prominently. This writer was fascinated by the fact that the Creator God of the Bible would have laid out in such specific terms — some 600 plus years before the birth of Jesus Christ — what he had planned throughout history.

However, unknown to him at that time, the interpretation of the **end** of Daniel's prophecy — as presented by those human individuals with whom this writer was dealing — created what amounted to a mental block; that obstacle was to remain in place for 25 years. Why? With virtually no historical or biblical background from which to analyze their conclusions, he was basically "programmed" to accept their opinions as "gospel." For years afterwards — as a result of accepting a number of premises which were fundamentally flawed — he inevitably reached false conclusions on this vital subject.

DANIEL

Although many readers will be familiar with much of the basic prophecy, it is good that we review it again briefly at this point.

Daniel was a young man who had been carried captive to Babylon during the reign of Jehoiakim. Although nothing is known of his family, Daniel is thought to have been of noble descent (*Daniel* 1:2). He and three companions — because of their special qualifications — were selected to be trained for the king's service (1:2,4). "God gave them knowledge and skill in all learning and wisdom: and Daniel had understanding in all visions and dreams" (v.17).

KING NEBUCHADNEZZAR'S DREAM

A few years later king Nebuchadnezzar had a vivid dream. Although it made a tremendous impression on him, the king claimed he couldn't remember the dream. When commanded by Nebuchadnezzar, his magicians, astrologers, and sorcerers were unable to tell him what he had dreamed. The king ordered them to be slain.

Shortly thereafter, Daniel — who was about to be killed with the rest of the king's counselors — had a vision in which God revealed to him the contents of the king's dream (*Daniel* 2:19). Daniel was brought before the king. Despite the inability of the Babylonian wise men to tell the king his dream, Daniel declared that "there is a God in heaven that reveals secrets, and makes known to the king Nebuchadnezzar what shall be in the latter days.... he that reveals secrets makes known to you what shall come to pass" (v.28,29).

Assuring the king that this secret was not revealed to him by any wisdom of his own (v.30), Daniel told him his dream. In it, the king had seen a great image which had a head of fine gold; its breast and arms were of silver; its belly and thighs were of brass. Its legs of iron, its feet part of iron and part of clay.

Suddenly there appeared a stone — as if from nowhere — that smashed the image on its feet and broke them in pieces. At that time "the iron, clay, brass, silver, and the gold were broken to pieces together, and became like the chaff on the summer threshingfloors; and the wind carried them away, and no place was found for them; and the stone that smote the image became a great mountain, and filled the whole earth" (vs.30-35).

In *Daniel* 7:1-8, the prophet had a dream and visions in which he saw the same events unfold, but from a very different perspective. In his vision, Daniel saw the various empires as they really were: wild beasts.

In verse 13 we read of the coming of "one like the son of man" (Christ, *Matthew* 8:20;9:6). "And there was given unto him dominion, and glory, and a kingdom, that all people, nations and languages should serve him: his dominion is an everlasting dominion, which shall not pass away, and his kingdom that which shall not be destroyed.

INTERPRETATION

The interpretation? Daniel identified Nebuchadnezzar as the head of gold to whom the God of heaven had given "a kingdom, power, and strength, and glory.... You are this head of gold" (*Daniel* 2:37,38).

Daniel continued: "And after you shall arise another kingdom inferior to you, and another third kingdom of brass which shall have rule over the whole earth" (v.39). History identifies these kingdoms as Medo-Persia (silver) and Greece (brass). The descending quality of the representative metals indicates a deterioration in the overall quality of the successive empires.

In about 538 B.C., the Babylonian Empire (which had been "weighed in the balance, and ... found wanting" — *Daniel* 5:27) was conquered in one night. While the king and his governors engaged in drunken debauchery, the Medo-Persians — led by Darius, who had diverted the river that ran through the city of Babylon — marched into

THE BIG SHOWDOWN

the metropolis along the dry river bed. The city was quickly overpowered.

Some years later, following the deaths of Philip of Macedon and his son Alexander the Great (under whose reign Medo-Persian power reached its zenith), the empire was divided into three separate parts — and immediately began to disintegrate.

In the ensuing 250-300 years (The Hellenistic Era), a cosmopolitan Greek-oriented culture held sway. The sciences thrived; fields of study included mathematics, astronomy, geography, medicine, and chemistry.

THE ROMAN EMPIRE

Again, Daniel continues: "And the fourth kingdom shall be strong as iron: forasmuch as iron breaks in pieces and subdues all things: and as iron that breaks all these, shall it break in pieces and bruise.

"And whereas you saw the feet and the toes, part of potters' clay, and part of iron, the kingdom shall be divided; but there shall be in it of the strength of the iron, forasmuch as you saw the iron mixed with miry clay.

"And as the toes of the feet were part of iron, and part of clay, so the kingdom shall be partly strong, and partly broken.

"And whereas you saw iron mixed with miry clay, they shall mingle themselves with the seed of men: but they shall not cleave one to another, even as iron is not mixed with clay" (*Daniel* 2:40-43).

This is, of course, the Roman Empire which began to develop some 250 years before Christ. Through military expansion and colonization, and by granting citizenship to conquered tribes, Rome's influence spread quickly. As a consequence of the three Punic Wars (264-146 B.C.), Rome took over from Greece and (representing the "iron" in Nebuchadnezzar's image) became the mightiest of the powers on the world scene up to that time. The Roman Empire conquered Gaul (France), Britain, and Europe up to the Danube. It lasted more than 500 years.

As prophesied by Daniel, the Roman Empire was partly strong and partly weak — just like "iron mixed with miry clay."

"IN THE DAYS OF THESE KINGS"

Up to this point there is little if any dispute among theologians or Bible students regarding the interpretation of Daniel's prophecy; it clearly relates to the four empires outlined above.

The "problem" arises with verse 44: "And in the days of those kingdoms **shall** the God of heaven set up a kingdom that **shall never** be destroyed: and the kingdom **shall not** be left to other people, but it **shall** break in pieces and consume all these kingdoms and it **shall** stand for ever." The next verse states that "the stone cut out of the mountain without hands ... broke in pieces the iron, the brass, the clay, the silver and the gold; the great God has made known to the king what **shall** come to pass hereafter: and the dream is certain, and the interpretation thereof sure."

Notice that the word **shall** is used six times in these two verses. God doesn't say he "hopes to" or "possibly may" do a number of things: he says he **shall** do them.

Most theologians and Bible students accept the fact that the "stone ... cut out without hands" (or without human assistance) mentioned here is in fact Jesus Christ. In scripture Jesus is referred to in that manner (see, *Matthew* 16:18; 21:42,44). In other words, the kingdom established by the God of heaven has nothing in common with the kingdoms or empires it replaces. It is totally separate from them.

A PROBLEM FOR MANY

The "problem" in the minds of many is when God **did** or **will do** what he says. Most pre-millennial dispensationalists, heavily influenced by the superabundant footnotes in their Scofield "bibles" believe that God decided to wait close to another 2,000 years (a mystery dispensation during which "the clock of prophecy was stopped") to set up his kingdom. Others believe that God set up his kingdom in the first century. What does the Bible say?

As we saw in a previous chapter, during his earthly ministry Jesus stated: "The time **is** fulfilled, and **the kingdom of heaven is at hand**: repent, and believe the gospel" (*Mark* 1:15). "[T]here be some of them that stand here who shall **not** see death till they **have** seen the kingdom of heaven **come** with power" (*Matthew* 9:1). Later in his ministry, Jesus also said: "The kingdom of God comes **not** with observation.... behold, **the kingdom of God is within you**" (*Luke* 17:20,21).

Following the death, resurrection and ascension of Jesus Christ, the apostle Paul stated: "The kingdom of God **is** [present tense] ... righteousness, and peace, and joy in the Holy [Spirit]" (*Romans* 14:17). "For the kingdom of God is **not** in word, but in power" (*I Corinthians* 4:20). He also declared that God "**has** [present tense] delivered us **from** the power of darkness, and **has** [present tense] translated us into the kingdom of his dear Son" (*Colossians* 1:13).

"TURNED THE WORLD UPSIDE DOWN"

The truth of those statements is reflected in the fact that — in the eyes of the Roman authorities — first-century Christians "turned the world upside down" because they had "another king, one Jesus" (*Acts* 17:6,7). Truly, they had been "translated into the kingdom" of Jesus Christ! It was their message that God is Sovereign and that Jesus Christ is Lord that not only "turned the world upside down" but also was instrumental, as prophesied in Daniel, in breaking in pieces and "blowing away" the series of world ruling empires that had existed from time immemorial.

In actual fact, in the first century the whole world had long-since been "upside down" as the result of being under Satan's control. When the gospel was preached — and as people's eyes and ears were opened to its awesome truths by the grace of God — it brought everything into proper perspective; lives were revolutionized — turned right side up!

That, in the eyes of a deceived world (*Revelation* 12:9), was tantamount to "turning the world upside down." The same attitude, of course, prevails today. To a world which prides itself on its ultra-sophistication [captious and fallacious reasoning], "anyone who believes in God is mentally ill" (Paul Brandwein, *The Social Sciences*, Harcourt Brace, 1970, p.10). There is nothing new under heaven!

It truly was in the days of those kings that the God of heaven set up his kingdom which shall never be destroyed (*Daniel* 2:44). Today, that kingdom is represented on earth by his church — his body. Those who are his true disciples "are ambassadors for Christ" (*I Corinthians* 12:20,27; *II Corinthians* 5:20). As Jesus confirmed during his ministry, "the gates of hell shall not prevail against it" (*Matthew* 16:18).

END TIME EVENTS

Where does all this leave us at the end of the twentieth century? What does the future hold? Is there a "more sure word of prophecy" (*II Peter* 1:19) to which we can look for guidance and support in these perilous times?

We turn once again to the book of Revelation — and a couple of visions that John saw. In chapter 13, we read that as John was standing upon the sand of the sea he saw a beast rising up out of the sea (water is a symbol for people and nations — *Revelation* 17:15). The beast had seven heads and ten horns. In *Revelation* 17:3, John had a similar vision; this time he saw a woman sitting upon a scarlet colored beast "having seven heads and ten horns." In verse 9 we are told that the seven heads represent seven kingdoms.

Now, notice verse 10. At the time John was writing (A.D. 94), he said there were "seven kings [i.e. kingdoms or empires]. Five are fallen, one is, and the other is not yet come; and when he comes he must continue a short space."

Which were the five world ruling empires that had "fallen" by the time John lived? Egypt, Assyria, Babylon, Medo-Persia, and Greece. Which one still existed in A.D. 94? Rome. The Roman Empire finally collapsed in A.D. 476.

Since the time of Christ — and following the fall of Rome — there have been no world-ruling empires. As prophesied in the book of *Daniel*, they had been broken up and blown away by the arrival of Christianity.

RESURRECTION OF ROMAN EMPIRE?

John tells us that, as of A.D. 94, another empire was to arise. Now, more than 1500 years after the collapse of the Roman Empire, there are definite signs that a seventh empire (or beast) may now be finally rising from the ashes of the old Roman Empire through the unification of Europe. It has the definite potential — through uniting with the other Trilateral powers — North America and Asia — of developing into a truly one world empire or New World Order.

Also today, for the first time in history, the technology — instant communications worldwide through satellites, faxes, modems, etc. — is available that would make this possible.

If, in fact, the seventh empire (or beast) is emerging at this time what characteristics should we look for in its formation? According to

Revelation 13:2, it should incorporate all of the strongest points that characterized each of the six empire that preceded it. Most important of all, we must recognize that it is the dragon (identified in chapter 12:3 as "Satan who deceives the whole world") which gives this beast "his power, and his seat, and great authority" (*Revelation* 13:2).

Verse 3 tells us that this is the resurrection of a system that had appeared to be dead. The population of the whole world is so awestricken at the appearance of this beast that they worship both the beast and the dragon (Satan) which gave it its power. The whole Satanic system appears so overwhelming and invincible that, in effect, they cry out: "Who is like unto the beast? Who is able to make war with him?" (v.4).

As was true with the first six empires, this seventh empire is adamantly opposed to the God of the Bible. Notice that in the working out of his purposes, God permits this: "There was **given** unto him [the beast] a mouth speaking great things and blasphemies; and power was **given** to him to continue forty and two months.

"And he opened his mouth in blasphemy against God, to blaspheme his name, and his tabernacle, and them that dwell in heaven" (vs.5,6).

Strong's Exhaustive Concordance of the Bible (reference #987) defines blasphemy as: "To vilify, to speak impiously, defame, rail on, revile, speak evil." In other words, the whole system is characterized by such activity.

Notice something else that God permits. "And it was **given** unto him [the beast] to make war with the saints and to overcome them: and power was **given** unto him over **all** kindreds, and tongues and nations." God permits Satan to persecute and temporarily overcome his people (those who have been redeemed by the blood of Christ, and saved by his life). He also permits Satan to create his New World Order which, humanly speaking, is invincible.

In verse 8 we read: "And **all** that dwell upon the earth **shall** worship him [the beast], whose names are **not** written in the book of life of the Lamb slain from the foundation of the world." Only those who have an "ear" will know and understand the message contained in this statement (v.9. See also *Revelation* 2:7,11; *John* 10:27).

WAR ON GOD

Until very recently the United States was recognized as a Christian nation. On three different occasions (1892, 1952, and 1961), the Supreme Court ruled it to be such.

Over the last three or four decades, however, we have seen ever-increasing — and ever more vicious — attacks on Christianity and the Bible. What was a strictly fringe movement in a sub-strata of American society early in the twentieth century has now developed into a dominant force in our national affairs.

The Bible has now been removed from all "public" (government-controlled, taxpayer-financed) schools. As we saw in chapter 11, the educational authorities believe that "any child who believes in God is mentally ill."

On the religious front the attack on Christianity and the Bible is led primarily by Talmudic Jews. One method of attack used is movie productions such *The Last Temptation of Christ* — a viciously blasphemous attack on Christ. Another is through articles and books. For example, while reviewing a book in *Midstream*, February/March 1996, Moshe Aberbach attacks the credibility of the Bible. Without giving any details, he refers to the alleged "discrepancies and contradictions with which the New Testament abounds ... [I]t is really impossible to make sense of the New Testament accounts of the origin of Christianity.... [N]o scholar who is looking for history rather than theology can possibly accept the gospel stories, with their logical absurdities, as authentic."

Aberbach then argues that Christianity must be false because, "The overwhelming majority of the vast literature was written by believing Christians who had a theological ax to grind.... Jesus was ... in fact a Kingdom of God agitator ... who engaged in seditious activities." He was "a rebel against `Caesar,' i.e. the Roman Emperor." And one last insult: Christ's "messianic movement [was] distinguished by its low-class devotees."

The purpose of such articles is, of course, to further undermine faith in God and his word, the Bible. The ultimate goal is best expressed in *Brain-Washing: A Synthesis of the Russian Textbook on Psychopolitics*: "We must recruit every agency of the nation slated for slaughter ... into foaming hatred of religion.... You must suborne district attorneys and judges into an intense belief that [Christianity] is ... bad, insanity producing, hated, and intolerable" (p.59). **Belief in God will be classified as insanity.**

HUMANISM REVEALS ITS ANTI-SUPERNATURALISTIC BIAS

Another public manifestation of such anti-supernaturalistic bias is *The Humanist Manifesto I & II*. We quote from the latter document: "[H]umanists ... believe that traditional theism ... is an unproved and outmoded faith.... Reasonable minds [like those posssessed by the Illuminated Ones?] look for other means for survival" (Preface). "[W]e must save ourselves" (p.14).

"The next century can be and should be the humanistic century ... we stand at the dawn of a new age.... Using technology wisely, we can ... provide humankind with unparellelled opportunity for achieving an abundant and meaningful life [That's exactly what Adam Weishaupt told his followers the Illuminati would provide].

"We believe [Humanism is a religious faith, see pp.1,8,9] ... that traditional dogmatic and authoritarian religions that place revelation, God, ritual, or creed above human needs and experience do a disservice to the human species" (pp.15-16).

"Ethics are authonomous, and situational, needing no theological or ideological sanction" (p.17).

Following the destruction of faith in a Creator God, what is the basic aim of the Humanists? Creation of a **one world government!** "We deplore the division of humankind on nationalistic grounds. We have reached a turning point in human history where the best option is to **transcend the limits of national sovereignty** and to **move toward the building of a world community**" (p.21).

"**A socialized and cooperative economic order must be established** to the end that the equitable distribution of the means of life be possible" (p.10).

The humanistic (man is "as god") state, which, as we saw earlier, has been given its "power ... and great authority" by Satan, has now taken the place of God in the lives of most. The state, "as god" (*Genesis* 3:5), provides for all their needs — from the cradle to the grave. In its new role, it is "worshipped" by most. "Who is like unto the beast?"

WHO IS THE EIGHTH BEAST?

Most premillennial dispensationalists — relying heavily, as usual, on the footnotes in their Scofield "bibles" — believe that Christ will return in the near future to defeat this seventh beast and thus establish his millennial reign on earth. This, they believe, will usher in an unprecedented golden age of peace and abundance.

For more than one hundred years premillennial dispensationalists have been spreading the belief that the seventh beast is the **final** anti-Christ, and that Christ will come to defeat him and thus establish his millennial kingdom on earth, with headquarters at Jerusalem. With a few minor variations, this basic scenario is believed by most — perhaps 80-85 percent — churchgoers today. A careful examination of scripture, however, reveals that such a belief system was unknown not only to the Christians of the first century, but to those who emerged following the Reformation.

A question. Could "that old serpent, called the Devil, and Satan, which deceives the whole world" (*Revelation* 12:9), be about to pull another "fast one" on the mesmerized millions that populate planet earth? That possibility arises when we consider a verse of scripture that is ignored by all but a few people; we refer to *Revelation* 17:11: "And the beast that was, and is not, even he is the eighth, **and is of the seven**, and goes into perdition."

Here we see an **eighth beast** which is not mentioned elsewhere. We are told he "is of the seven." In other words, the eighth beast belongs to the same old Luciferian/Egyptian/Babylonian system as all the others. But, being "the eighth," he is obviously other than and apart from the seventh. They are not one and the same.

Who could this eighth beast be? The Scofieldite premilleniaI dispensationalists choose to ignore the eighth beast; it isn't mentioned in any of their literature. Adhering to their footnotes, they expect Christ to return bodily to earth in order to crush the seventh beast and then set up a physical kingdom, headquartered in Jerusalem.

As no such scenario appears in scripture, is it possible that the Scofieldites may have been taken in by — and fallen for — a diversionary tactic that is destined to rock the world to its foundations in the years immediately ahead?

Bearing in mind that it is Satan who gives the seventh beast "his power and great authority" (*Revelation* 13:2), is it possible that Satan is preparing a decoy to take the fall in a much more spectactular power grab?

As we saw in chapter 5, **Satan is insatiable in his lust for power**. The prophet Isaiah lays bare Satan's awesome ambitions: "For you [Lucifer, or Satan] have said in your heart, **I will** ascend into [or in] heaven, **I will** exalt my throne [position of rulership] above the stars [angels, *Revelation* 1:20]; **I will** sit upon the mount of the congregation, in the sides of the north:

"**I will** ascend above the heights of the clouds; **I will** be like the most High" (vs.13,14).

Clearly, Satan wants to take over from God. That is his all-consuming goal. And in these last days he believes he has a fail-proof opportunity to do just that. **But how?**

A PHONY "SECOND COMING"?

The idea of such a "kingdom of heaven on earth" had been considered as a possibility by a small minority since about the time of Christ. It only began to emerge and grow when combined with the "pre-trib" rapture doctrine; the latter was based on "visions" that sprang into the mind of a young Scottish girl, Margaret Macdonald, in 1830. These errors were heavily promoted by John Darby, Edward Irving, Ethelbert W. Bullinger, C.I. Scofield, and others. Both now form the basis for what is currently known as "premillennial dispensationalism," that is, that Jesus Christ will establish a kingdom here on earth.

This writer believes that this doctrine is, in fact, a Satanic counterfeit — a diabolical masterpiece of Luciferian ingenuity — introduced by demonic forces to set the stage for Satan's ultimate grab for total power? Fantastic? Don't be too sure!

As these two false doctrines are so deeply ingrained in the minds of so many nominal Christians today, is it possible that Satan will stage a phony — **but extremely convincing** — "return of Christ to earth" in order to wipe out the seventh beast and set up a counterfeit "kingdom of heaven," with headquarters in Jerusalem? Hundreds of millions — possibly billions — could thus be deceived into believing that the Christ of the Bible has actually returned to establish his kingdom as forecast in the footnotes of the Scofield "bible."

Particularly when considered in the light of what Christ said in his Olivet discourse, it emerges as a distinct possibility: "For there **shall** arise false Christs, and false prophets, and **shall show great signs and wonders; insomuch that, if it were possible, they shall deceive the very elect**" (*Matthew* 24:24).

Truly, such a staggering event could, if it were possible, deceive even the very elect of God!

Further weight is given to the idea of a false kingdom when we consider the passage of scripture from *Revelation* 13 which we quoted earlier regarding the emergence of the seventh, or endtime, beast that emerged "from the sea." (As already shown, the sea or water symbolizes the nations of the earth).

In verse 11 we read of "another beast coming up **out of the earth**." Apparently when this beast emerges on the world scene the nations have already been merged into one unit (the New World Order?), symbolized by the solid, immoveable "earth." Notice that this new arrival **looks** like a lamb (Christ), but speaks like a dragon (Satan). Here, the Bible clearly portrays Satan as imitating Christ, and doing what many nominal Christians expect Christ to do: destroy what many consider to be the "anti-Christ" and then establish his "millennial kingdom" on earth. **Obviously, as this deceives everyone but "the very elect"** — those who are sealed by the Holy Spirit — **it must be the smoothest con job in history!**

Read on, and see what this phony "Christ" does to demonstrate his power and authority. Among other things, "He exercises all the power of the first beast before him, and causes the earth and them that dwell therein to **worship** the first beast [**now posing as the kingdom of God**?] whose deadly wound was healed." In addition, "he does great wonders ... and deceives them that dwell on the earth by the means of those miracles which he has power to do in the sight of the first beast" (vs.12-14).

Remember, people who are deceived don't know they are deceived. They may be both totally sincere — and totally deceived — at the same time.

AIMS OF TALMUDIC ZIONISM

This possible scenario is also in line with the goals and aims of Talmudic Zionism which despises Jesus Christ and everything he represents. The Jewish *Babylonian Talmud* states that Jesus was a bastard and that his mother, Mary, was a whore. It also declares that Jesus is "a bloody and deceitful man" who is presently "boiling in hot excrement." See this author's book, *Anti-Semitism and the Babylonian Connection*, for full documentation — and more!

In 1962, former Israeli prime minister David Ben Gurion, looked forward to the time when "All armies will be abolished, and there will be no more wars. **In Jerusalem**, the United Nations (a truly *United* Nations) will build a shrine to the Prophets to serve the federated union of all continents; **this will be the seat of the Supreme Court of Mankind**, to settle all controversies among the federated continents, **as prophesied by Isaiah**" (*Look magazine*, January 16, 1962, p.20).

According to Tommy Baer, international president of B'nai B'rith, the largest Jewish organization in the world, this planned world government headquartered in Jerusalem represents "the ultimate Messianic Age that both Christians **and Jews** look forward to with hope and faith" (Letter to Morris Chapman, president of the Executive Committee, Southern Baptist Convention, summer 1996).

As scripture asks: "Can two walk together, except they be agreed?" (*Amos* 3:3). Can those who are clearly dedicated to an "anti-Christ" worldview also be dedicated to something that is truly Christian and biblical in origin? Obviously not!

But as Jesus Christ, the true Messiah, declared: "If it were possible, they shall deceive the very elect" (*Matthew* 24:24).

A STAGED EVENT?

How could such a power grab be staged effectively? Let's review some current world order activities which may point toward the preparation of a mass deception. One possibility is that a planned phony "return of Christ" may be tied into the strange goings-on (UFOs and other aerial phenomena) observed and filmed around top-secret facilities such as Groom Lake (Area 51) some 100 miles north of Las Vegas, Nevada, and at four facilities in the Palmdale/Lancaster/Arvin (Bakersfield) areas north of Los Angeles where development of flying saucers and related technology is taking place. (For information on Groom Lake, see the video, *The Panic Project*, available from Emissary Publications).

Such a power grab could be staged through the use of space platforms in orbit 100-200 miles above the face of the earth. Through the use of modern technology — holographic images, lasers, and as-yet-undisclosed special effects, and with the full cooperation of all the television networks — such a scenario is well within the realm of possibility.

This writer has learned from a man who recently lost his high-paying, top-security job with a major defence contractor in Florida as a result of being too inquisitive, that one ultra top-secret project under development is known as "New Jerusalem." Although he never got close enough to discover exactly what this hush-hush project is all about, he believes it has to do with space platforms now under development in the near reaches of space.

Regardless of how it comes down, there will also be endtime manifestations such as the apostle Paul warned about when he spoke of "another Jesus ... another spirit ... [and] another gospel." "Satan himself [will be] **transformed into an angel of light**" [Remember Jesus said, "I am the light" — *John* 14:6]. Also, "his [Satan's] ministers [will also] transform themselves **as** the ministers of righteousness." There will be "false apostles, deceitful workers [who will] transform themselves into the apostles of Christ" (*II Corinthians* 11:13-15).

The Bible also indicates that some of Satan's human instrumentalities will be embodied by both Satan and his top lieutenants.

What happens next? As Satan (a.k.a. Lucifer) wants to be "like the most High," he moves to put his seal or "mark" on "both small and great, rich and poor, free and bond." The reader will remember that God has already sealed or marked his people — his elect (*Revelation* 7:3-8).

As was true in the old Testament, when Satan repeatedly attempted to wipe out the seed line that would eventually lead to the birth of Jesus Christ, so also in these last days he will strive mightily to erase God's elect — his church — from the face of the earth.

In *Revelation* 17:6 the whole Babylonian system is portrayed as being "drunken with the blood of the saints, and with the blood of the martyrs of Jesus." Then, in *Revelation* 6:9 we see a picture of an altar under which were "the souls of them [in Christ] which were slain for the word of God, and for the testimony which they held."

In another scripture, we see those who have been martyred for Christ crying out to God for justice to be done: "How long, O Lord, holy and true do you not judge and avenge our blood on them that dwell on the earth?" (*Revelation* 6:10). They know that as he is "Holy and True " — and thus a totally law-abiding and just God — he will not allow these terrible crimes to go unpunished forever. If he did, he wouldn't truly be God.

"THE GATES OF HELL SHALL NOT PREVAIL AGAINST IT"

In God's word, however, we have the blessed assurance that the "gates of hell shall not prevail against it." The church will never be destroyed or completely die out. Just before the second coming of Christ, we are told that he "shall gather together his elect from the four winds, from the uttermost part of the earth to the uttermost part of heaven" (*Mark* 13:27). Through the resurrection power of Jesus Christ, they will storm the gates of hell (the grave) to be with their Redeemer, Savior, and King when he finally steps in to put an end to Satan's rebellion and deception.

And then? Back to Revelation 17 and the eighth beast and his cohorts: "These have one mind, and shall give their power and strength unto the [eighth] beast. These shall make war with the Lamb, and the Lamb shall overcome them: **for he is Lord of lords, and King of kings, and they that are with him are called, and chosen, and faithful**" (17:13,14).

Another view of this scenario appears in chapter 19: here, Christ appears as the one called "Faithful and True, and in righteousness he does judge and make war." He is followed by those who are "clothed in fine linen, white and clean."

"Out of **his** mouth goes a sharp sword, that with it **he** should smite the nations, and he shall rule them with a rod of iron: and he treads the winepress of the fierceness and wrath of Almighty God.

"And he has on his vesture, and on his thigh a name written, KING OF KINGS AND LORD OF LORDS" (vs. 11,14,15,16).

"At the name of Jesus, every knee shall bow ... and every tongue ... confess that Jesus Christ is Lord, to the glory of God the Father" (*Philippians* 2:10,11).

"Death is swallowed up in victory. O death, where is your sting? O grave, where is your victory?.... [T]hanks be to God who gives us the victory through Jesus Christ our Lord.

"Therefore, my beloved brethren, be you steadfast, **unmovable**, always **abounding in the work of the Lord**, forasmuch as you know that **your labor is not in vain in the Lord**" (*I Corinthians* 15:54,55, 57,58).

As Jesus Christ instructs: "Occupy till I come" (*Luke* 19:13).

To Stand Alone

It is human to stand with the crowd, it is Divine to stand alone. It is man-like to follow the people, to drift with the tide; it is God-like to follow a principle, to stem the tide.

It is natural to compromise conscience and follow the social and religious fashion for the sake of gain or pleasure; it is divine to sacrifice both on the altar of truth and duty.

"No man stood with me, but all men forsook me," wrote the battle-scarred apostle in describing his first appearance before Nero to answer for his life for believing and teaching contrary to the Roman world.

Truth has been out of fashion since man changed his robe of fadeless light for a garment of faded leaves.

Noah built and voyaged alone. His neighbors laughed at his strangeness and perished in style.

Abraham wandered and worshipped alone. Sodomites smiled at the simple shepherd, followed the fashion, and fed the flames.

Daniel dined and prayed alone. Elijah sacrificed and witnessed alone. Jeremiah prophesied and wept alone. Jesus loved and died alone.

Of the lonely way His disciples should walk, He said: "Strait is the gate and narrow the way which leads unto life and few there be that find it."

Of their treatment by the many who walk in the broad way, He said, "If you were of the world, the world would love his own; but because you are not of the world, therefore the world hates you."

The church in the wilderness praised Abraham and persecuted Moses. The Church of the Kings praised Moses and persecuted the prophets.

The Church of Caiphas praised the prophets and persecuted Jesus. The Church of the Popes praised the Savior and persecuted the saints. And multitudes now, in the Church and in the world, applaud the courage of the patriarchs and prophets, the apostles and martyrs, but condemn as stubbornness or foolishness, like faithfulness today.

WANTED TODAY, men and women, young and old, who will obey their convictions of truth and duty at the cost of fortune and friends and life itself.

— Author Unknown.

Postscript

ENCOURAGING THE REMNANT

By Albert J. Nock

One evening last autumn, I sat long hours with a European acquaintance while he expounded a politico-economic doctrine which seemed sound as a nut and with which I could find no defect. At the end, he said with great earnestness: "I have a mission to the masses. I feel I am called to get the ear of the people. I shall devote the rest of my life to spreading my doctrine far and wide among the populace. What do you think?"

An embarrassing question in any case, and doubly so under the circumstances. My acquaintance is a very learned man, one of the three or four really first-class minds that Europe produced in his generation. Naturally I, as one of the unlearned, was inclined to regard his lightest word with reverence amounting to awe.

ISAIAH'S JOB

I referred him to the story of the prophet Isaiah. I shall paraphrase the story in our common speech since it has to be pieced together from various sources.

The prophet's career began at the end of King Uzziah's reign, say about 740 B.C. This reign was uncommonly long (almost half a century) and apparently prosperous. It was one of those prosperous reigns, however — like the reign of Marcus Aurelius at Rome, or the administration of Eubulus at Athens, or of Mr. Coolidge at Washington — where, at the end, the prosperity suddenly peters out and things go by the board with a resounding crash.

In the year of Uzziah's death, the Lord commissioned the prophet to go out and warn the people of the wrath to come: "*Tell them what a worthless lot they are,*" He said. "*Tell them what is wrong, and why, and what is going to happen unless they have a change of heart and straighten up. Don't mince matters. Make it clear that they are positively down to their last chance. Give it to them good and strong, and keep giving it to them.*

"I suppose I ought to tell you," He added, "*that it won't do any good. The official class and their intelligentsia will turn up their noses at you, and the masses will not even listen. They will all keep on in their own ways until they carry everything down to destruction, and you will probably be lucky if you get out of it with your life.*"

Isaiah had been willing to take on the job. In fact, he had asked for it. But the prospect put a new face on the situation. It raised the obvious question: Why, if all that were so — if the enterprise were to be a failure from the start — was there any sense in starting it?

"Ah," the Lord said, you do not get the point. There is a remnant there that you know nothing about. They are obscure, unorganized, inarticulate, each one rubbing along as best he can. They need to be encouraged and braced up because when everything has gone completely to the dogs, they are the ones who will come back and build up a new society. Meanwhile, your preaching will reassure them and keep them hanging on. Your job is to take care of the Remnant, so be off and set about it."

THE GREAT MEDIOCRE MASSES

What do we mean by the masses, and by the Remnant? As the word "masses" is commonly used, it suggests agglomerations of poor and underprivileged people, laboring people, the proletarians. But it means nothing like that. *It means simply the majority.* The mass-man has neither the force of intellect to apprehend the principles issuing in what we know as the humane life, nor the force of character to adhere to those principles steadily and strictly as laws of conduct. Because such people make up the great, the overwhelming majority of mankind, they are called, collectively, the masses. The line of differentiation between the masses and the Remnant is set invariably by quality, not by circumstances. The Remnant are those who, by force of intellect, are able to apprehend these principles, and by force of character are able, at least measurably, to cleave to them. The masses are those who are unable to do either.

The picture which Isaiah presents of the Judean masses is most unfavorable. In his view, the mass-man (be he high or be he lowly, rich or poor, prince or pauper) gets off very badly. He appears as not only weak-minded and weak-willed, but as by consequence knavish, arrogant, grasping, dissipated, unprincipled, unscrupulous.

SEEKING MASS ACCEPTANCE

As things now stand, Isaiah's job seems rather to go begging. *Everyone with a message nowadays is, like my venerable European friend, eager to take it to the masses.* His first, last, and only thought is of mass-acceptance and mass-approval. His great care is to put his doctrine in such a shape as will capture the masses' attention and interest.

The main problem with this [mass-man] approach is its reaction upon the mission itself. It necessitates an opportunistic sophistication of one's doctrine, which profoundly alters its character and reduces it to a mere placebo. If, say, you are a preacher, you wish to attract as large a congregation as you can. This means an appeal to the masses; and this, in turn, *means adapting the terms of your message to the order of intellect and character that the masses exhibit.* If you are an educator, say with a college on your hands, you wish to get as many students as possible, and you whittle down your requirements accordingly. If a writer, you aim at getting many readers. If a publisher, many purchasers. If a philosopher, many disciples. If a reformer, many converts, and so on. But as you see all sides, in the realization of these several desires, the prophetic message is so heavily adulterated with trivialities, in every instance, that its effect on the masses is merely to harden them in their sins. *Meanwhile, the Remnant, aware of this adulteration and the desires that prompt it, turn their backs on the prophet and will have nothing to do with him or his message.*

Isaiah, on the other hand, worked under no such disabilities. He preached to the masses only in the sense that he preached publicly. Anyone who liked might listen. Anyone who liked might pass by. *He knew the Remnant would listen.*

WHO AND WHERE ARE THE REMNANT?

The Remnant want only the best you have, whatever that may be. Give them that and they are satisfied; you have nothing more to worry about. In a sense, nevertheless, as I have said, it is not a rewarding job. A prophet to the Remnant will not grow purse-proud from the returns from his work, nor is it likely that he will get any great renown out of it. Isaiah's case was exceptional to this second rule. There are others, but not many!

OTHER COMPENSATIONS

It may be thought, then, that while taking care of the Remnant is no doubt a good job, it is not an especially interesting job because it is as a rule so poorly paid. I have my doubts about this. There are others compensations to be got out of a job besides money and notoriety. Some of these are substantial enough to be attractive. Many jobs that do not pay well are yet profoundly interesting, as, for instance, the job of the research student in the sciences is said to be. The job of looking after the Remnant seems to me, as I survey it from my seat in the grandstand, to be as interesting as any that can be found in the world.

AN UNKNOWN QUANTITY

What chiefly makes it so, I think, is that in any given society the *Remnant are always an unknown quantity.* You do not know, and will never know, more than two things about them. You can be sure of those, but you will never to able to make even a respectable guess at anything else. You do not know, and will never know, who the Remnant are, nor where they are, nor what they are doing or will do. *Two things you know and no more: First, they exist; second, they will find you.* Except for these two certainties, working for the Remnant means working in impenetrable darkness. And this, I should say, is just the condition calculated most effectively to pique the interest of any prophet who is properly gifted with the imagination, insight, and intellectual curiosity necessary to a successful pursuit of his trade.

RIGHT-THINKING SUBSTRATUM

The fascination — as well as the despair — of the historian, as he looks back on Isaiah's Jewry, upon Plato's Athens, or upon Rome of the Antonines, is the hope of discovering and laying bare the "substratum of right-thinking and right-doing" which he knows must have existed somewhere in those societies, because no kind of collective life can possibly go on without it. He finds tantalizing imitations of it here and there in many places, as in the Greek anthology, in the scrapbook of Aulus Gellius, in the poems of Ausonius, and in the brief and touching tribute, *Bene merenti*, bestowed upon the unknown occupants of Roman tombs. But these are vague and fragmentary; they lead him nowhere in his search for some kind of measure of the substratum, but merely testify to what he already knew *a priori* — that the substratum did somewhere exist. Where it was, how substantial it was, what its power of self-assertion and resistance was — of all this they tell him nothing.

TWO THOUSAND YEARS HENCE

Similarly, when the historian of two thousand years hence, or two hundred years, looks over the available testimony to the quality of our civilization and tries to get any kind of clear, competent evidence of the stratum of right-thinking and well-doing which he knows must have been here, he will have a devil of a time finding it. When he has assembled all he can get and has made even a minimum allowance for speciousness, vagueness and confusion of motive, he will sadly acknowledge that his net result is exactly nothing. A Remnant were here, building a substratum like coral insects. So much he knows, but he will find nothing to put him on the track of who, and where, and how many they were, and what their work was like.

THE REMNANT IS LARGER THAN YOU THINK

Concerning all this, too, the prophet of the present knows precisely as much and as little as the historians of the future. And that, I repeat, is what makes his job seem to me so profoundly interesting. One of the most suggestive episodes recounted in the Bible is that of a prophet's attempt — the only attempt of the kind on record, I believe — to count up the Remnant. Elijah had fled from persecution into the desert, where the Lord presently overhauled him and asked him what he was doing so far away from his job. He said that he was running away, not because he was a coward, but because all the Remnant had been killed off except himself. He got away only by the skin of his teeth, and, he being now all the Remnant there was, if he were killed the True Faith would go flat.

The Lord replied that he need not worry about that, for even without him the True Faith would probably manage to squeeze along somehow if it had to. "And as for your figures on the Remnant," He said, "I don't mind telling you that there are seven thousand of them back there in Israel whom, it seems, you have not heard of, but you may take my word for it that they are there."

At that time, probably the population of Israel could not have run to much more than a million or so; and a Remnant of seven thousand out of a million is a highly encouraging percentage for any prophet. With seven thousand of the boys on his side, there was no great reason for Elijah to feel lonesome; and incidentally, that would be something for the modern prophet of the Remnant to think of when he has a touch of the blues. But the main point is that if Elijah the prophet could not make a closer guess on the number of the Remnant than he made when he missed it by seven thousand, any one else who tackled the problem would only waste his time.

THE REMNANT WILL FIND HIM

The other certainty that the prophet of the Remnant may always have is that the Remnant will find him. He may rely on that with absolute assurance. They will find him without him doing anything about it. In fact, if he tries to do anything about it, he is pretty sure to put them off. He does not need to advertise for them or to resort to any schemes of publicity to get their attention. If he is a preacher or a public speaker, for example, he may be quite indifferent to going on show at receptions, getting his pictures printed in the newspapers, or furnishing biographical material for publication on the side of "human interest." If a writer, he may not make a point of attending any pink teas, autographing books at wholesale, nor entering into any specious freemasonry with reviewers.

All this and much more of the same lies in the regular and necessary routine laid down for the prophet of the masses. It is, and must be, part of the great general technique of getting the mass-man's ear — or as our vigorous and excellent publicist H.L. Mencken, put it, the technique of "boob-bumping." The prophet of the masses is not bound to this technique. He may be quite sure that the Remnant will make their own way to him without any adventitious aids. *Not only so, but if they find him employing such aids, it is ten to one they will smell a rat in them and will shear off.*

The certainty that the Remnant will find him, however, leaves the prophet as much in the darkness as ever, as helpless as ever in the matter of putting any estimate of any kind upon the Remnant; for, as appears in the case of Elijah, he remains ignorant of who they are that have found him or where they are, or how many. They do not write in and tell him about it, after the manner of those who admire the vedettes of Hollywood, nor do they yet seek him out and attach themselves to his person. *They are not that kind. They take his message much as drivers take the directions on a roadside signpost — that is, with very little thought about the signpost, beyond being gratefully glad that it happened to be there, but with very serious thought about the directions.*

WILL SEE HIS MESSAGE REFLECTED

This impersonal attitude of the Remnant wonderfully enhances the interest of the imaginative prophet's job. Once in a while, just about often enough to keep his intellectual curiosity in good working order, he will quite accidentally come upon some distinct reflection of his own message in an unsuspected quarter. This enables him to entertain himself in his leisure moments with agreeable speculations about the course his message may have taken in reaching that particular quarter, and about what came of it once it got there. Most interesting of all are those instances, if one could only run them down (but one may always speculate about them), where the recipient himself no longer knows where, nor when, nor from whom he got his message. Or even where, as sometimes happens, he has forgotten that he got it anywhere and imagines that it is all a self-sprung idea of his own.

Such instances as these are probably not infrequent, for, without presuming to enroll ourselves among the Remnant, we can all no doubt remember having found ourselves suddenly under the influence of an idea, the source of which we cannot possibly identify. "It came to us afterwards," as we say. That is, we are aware of it only after it has shot up full-grown into our minds, leaving us quite ignorant of how, and when, and by what agency it was planted there and left to germinate. It seems highly probable that the prophet's message often takes some such course with the Remnant.

If, for example, you are a writer or a speaker, or a preacher, you put forth an idea which lodges in the mind of a casual member of the Remnant and sticks fast there. For some time it is inert. Then it begins to fret and fester until presently it invades the man's conscious mind and, as one might say, corrupts it. Meanwhile, he has quite forgotten how he came by the idea in the first instance, and even perhaps thinks he invented it. *In those circumstances, the most interesting thing of all is that you never know what the pressure of that idea will make him do.* ■

(The above was originally published in *The Freeman*, Irvington-on-Hudson, New York, NY 10533. Used by permission).

Index

Abraham, 13-14, 108-123, 133, 145, 182
Abrahamic Covenant, 163
Abraham's Seed, 110, 117, 149
Adam and Eve, 25-27
Age of Aquarius, 3
Amazing Grace, 134, 135
American Dictionary of the English Language, 21, 46
Anglo-American Establishment, 80
Anstey, Martin, 158
Babylon, 12
Balance of power, 63
Book of Revelation, 137
"British Race Patriots," 85
British Crown, 71-73
Church incorporation, 101, 102
Coolidge, Calvin 73
Cycle of failure, 27
Darwin, Charles, 8, 86
De Tocqueville, Alexis, 7, 16, 102, 104
Empire of the City, 64
French Revolution, 57
Garden of Eden, 25-27, 37
"Give us a king," 15
Groom Lake, 179
Illiminati, 52-58, 61, 88, 107, 127, 175
Jerusalem, 115, 148, 157-159, 176-179
  New, 108, 180
  Seige of, 16, 160
Johnson, Lyndon B., 76
Knuth, E. C., 63
Law of biogenesis, 132
Lincoln, Abraham, 5, 62, 71
Machievelli, 64
Man's heart, 28
Millennium, 108, 109, 170-178
  New, 3, 18, 64
Morals and Dogma, 89
New Age, 3
New Age Magazine, 82-83
New covenant, 154, 163
New world order, 2-5, 18, 42, 52, 63, 71, 86, 128, 166
Nimrod, 10, 12, 40-
Noah's Ark, 11

One-Hundred-and-Forty-Four-Thousand, 143
Pike, Albert, 81, 89
Pilgrim Society, 65
Proofs of a Conspiracy, 55
Quigley, Carroll, 66, 72, 80, 86, 166
Religion, 93
Repentance?, 131
Report From Iron Mountain, 74
Return of Christ, 176-179
Robison, John, 54
Roman Empire, 169, 172, 182
Roosevelt, Franklin D., 1848, 62, 76, 78, 80
"Salt of the earth," 7, 99, 142
Satan's world system, 39
Saving your "life", 31
Scofield, 104, 158 170, 176
Seventy Weeks, 154
Sovereign Grace, 31, 47, 116, 120, 129, 155
Sovereignty of God, 6, 18, 92, 103, 156, 171
Stanton, Edwin, 62
Talmud, 116, 117, 174
Talmudic Zionism, 178
Tragedy and Hope, 66, 72, 80
Tribes of Israel, 144
True doctrine forsaken, 104
True Israelites, 121, 149
Two Babylons, The, 12
United Nations plan, 84
Way to God, 127
Webster, Nesta, 55
Weishaupt, Adam, 51-56, 127,175
What is man?, 20
World War I, 70

Emissary Publications
FREE CATALOG:
We specialize in Books,
Tapes and Videos on
Globalism, Politics, History
Ecomnomics, and Religion.

Give Copies Of —

Storming the Gates of Hell

To Your Friends!

Order multiple copies at these special prices:

    1-2 copies $10.00 each
      3-5 copies $8.50
      6-9 copies $8.00
    10-19 copies $7.00
    20-29 copies $6.00
    30-39 copies $6.60
    40-49 copies $6.30
    50+ copies $5.00

Shipping & Handling:
$1.00 to $25.00 $2.50
Over $25.00   10% of Total Amount

Emissary Publications
9205 SE Clackamas Rd. SE, #1776
Clackamas, OR 97015

Fourth Reich Of The Rich

Descent Into Slavery?

$11.00 $11.00

By Des Griffin

Des Griffin takes over where other writers on the International Conspiracy leave off, bringing his readers behind the scenes in international politics and into the diabolical world of the Illuminati, the most secret of the secret societies.

In these fast moving, easy-to-read books, the author traces the history of the conspiracy down through the centuries and presents irrefutable documentation that will both shock and amaze you.

From the pages of *Fourth Reich* and *Descent Into Slavery?* pour facts that open up new vistas of understanding and make world affairs leap into life and become truly meaningful.

No wonder these books are winning acclaim worldwide:

"*Fourth Reich* is superb and should be used as a textbook in schools around the world," writes Count Sixtus von Plettenberg, economist, Germany.

In *Descent Into Slavery?* no punches are pulled by the author as he presents startling new documentation and brings his readers face-to-face with the raw realities of power politics. The inside story of World War II is truly eye-opening!

Anti-Semitism And The Babylonian Connection

E-103 $6.00

Des Griffin — ANTI-SEMITISM. That word strikes stark terror into the hearts and minds of many. Most will go to practically any lengths to avoid being smeared as "anti-Semitic."

Who is a Semite? Are all Jews Semites? What IS anti-Semitism? Is Judaism the God-centered religion of the Old Testament? What is Pharisaism? How important is the Babylonian Talmud to modern Jews? How did the Talmud come into being? What does it teach regarding Jews — and non-Jews?

Are those people who ask ANY valid questions regarding the Jews and Judaism, wicked, nasty and evil — and worthy of being ostracized, socially?

Des Griffin believes that all these questions — and more — must be addressed honestly and freely in an open forum.

Delving into Biblical and secular history, and a wide variety of Jewish sources stretching back more than 2300 years, Des Griffin has come up with a truly enthralling book — one that is exciting, explosive, and revealing! This book will CHALLENGE you. It will make you think about, and ponder many factors you may previously have been unaware of.

ANTI-SEMITISM: And The Babylonian Connection is a book for TODAY. It addresses the issues of today head on. It is packed with thoroughly documented facts, with insights and understanding that will give you a totally new perspective on the world in which we live.

Emissary Publications
9205 SE Clackamas Rd. SE, #1776
Clackamas, OR 97015